Bantam Books by Elisabeth Bing

MOVING THROUGH PREGNANCY
SIX PRACTICAL LESSONS FOR AN EASIER
CHILDBIRTH

SIX PRACTICAL LESSONS FOR AN EASIER CHILDBIRTH

Revised Edition

by Elisabeth Bing

Photographs by Norman McGrath
Drawings by Howard S. Friedman

BANTAM BOOKS · TORONTO · NEW YORK · LONDON

SIX PRACTICAL LESSONS FOR AN EASIER CHILDBIRTH

*A Bantam Book / published by arrangement with
the author*

PRINTING HISTORY

Grosset edition published March 1967

2nd printing .... March 1969   3rd printing .... June 1969

An excerpt appeared in EXPECTING *under the title
"The Lamaze Method" 1967*

Bantam edition / October 1969

2nd printing .... April 1970	6th printing .... March 1972
3rd printing .... November 1970	7th printing .... October 1972
4th printing .... June 1971	8th printing .... April 1973
5th printing .... November 1971	9th printing .... November 1973

Revised Bantam edition / March 1977

2nd printing .... May 1977	4th printing .... July 1978
3rd printing .... October 1977	5th printing ...... November 1978
6th printing .... June 1979

*The author and publisher thank Bill and Gail Meckel for
their good-natured assistance in the preparation of this book.*

ISBN 0-553-12216-9

Published simultaneously in the United States and Canada

*Bantam Books are published by Bantam Books, Inc. Its trade-
mark, consisting of the words "Bantam Books" and the por-
trayal of a bantam, is Registered in U.S. Patent and Trademark
Office and in other countries. Marca Registrada. Bantam
Books, Inc., 666 Fifth Avenue, New York, New York 10019.*

PRINTED IN THE UNITED STATES OF AMERICA

0 9 8 7 6

This book is dedicated to all the young parents who have studied with me, and to the memory of Marjorie Karmel.

Introduction

I wrote the first edition of this book exactly ten years ago, and not in my wildest dreams would I have ever thought that years later, this little textbook could still be in demand and be of practical help to thousands of young parents. Of course, I personally was convinced of the value of the Lamaze method but had simply hoped that "Prepared Childbirth" was here to stay and that its obvious appeal to parents would establish it as a "way of birth," not as some kind of fad of the sixties.

The Lamaze method has now become an accepted modality of obstetric procedure in our time. Today, hardly anyone will argue that it is detrimental to a woman's health or could endanger the newborn. And just because it has proved to be of lasting value, it has also proved to be a living tool. Changes have occurred, changes in technique to some extent, changes in approach, changes in obstetric knowledge; it is as if the infant Lamaze method has grown into early adulthood and that its existence is now taken for granted.

I had been asked for a number of years by many of my colleagues and also by my students, to revise this basic textbook, to bring it up to date (with completely new photographs of the exercises) and to reflect present obstetrical thinking. I would like to thank my editor at Bantam Books, Grace Bechtold, for helping me to describe these changes and to convince Bantam to publish this "growing child" so that it can be of as much help today to as many or more young parents as it has been for the last ten years.

Contents

Foreword
by Alan F. Guttmacher, M.D.

xi

Preface
by Heinz Luschinsky, M.D.

xiii

Our Class Convenes

An introduction to the lessons.
How do we control pain? How well does it work?

1

LESSON 1

How your body changes during pregnancy;
the importance of good posture;
the first stage of labor; the second stage of labor;
the third stage of labor.

13

LESSON 2

The neuromuscular control exercises;
the body-building exercises.

31

LESSON 3

Review; the three phases of early labor;
the first technique of breathing for early labor;

what to do with your hands; hyperventilation;
the position of your body during early labor;
the husband's role during practice at home.

57

LESSON 4

Review; back labor; ways to alleviate back
labor; the second breathing technique; using the
second breathing technique in labor; how your
husband can simulate a contraction; the transition;
the technique of breathing during transition.

75

LESSON 5

Review; the second stage of labor, or "expulsion";
the preliminary expulsion exercises;
what happens during actual delivery;
an exercise to prepare for delivery; the husband's
role during expulsion; the delivery-room table;
how to stop pushing on command.

93

LESSON 6

Recognizing the first signs of real labor;
breaking of waters; what to do when contractions
begin; what to take to the hospital; arriving
at the hospital; breathing with your labor;
the use of medication; beginning to push;
your baby arrives; after you've given birth.

105

A Mother's Report

125

A Father's Report

133

Foreword

Having begun obstetrics more than forty years ago, I have been privileged to witness a revolution in both its practice and its art. The revolution in practice was brought about through the wider use of prenatal care, transfusion and diagnostic X-ray, and by the introduction of improved anesthesia, better surgical techniques, chemotherapeutics and antibiotics. These improvements in practice produced a startling reduction in illness and death. In my early years we witnessed sixty-seven mothers die per ten thousand births; today less than three deaths occur in ten thousand births.

Change in the art has transformed childbirth from a grim, frightening experience into a happy, cheerful event. One may question why the change did not come sooner. Perhaps because the danger intrinsic in childbirth caused a fanatical concentration on safe deliverance. Then, when safety was accomplished, medicine relaxed its single focus and began to view the non-organic, the psychological aspects of childbirth. Grantly Dick-Read deserves credit for first emphasizing the harmful effects of fear and ignorance, both of which he attempted to dispel. His introduction of natural childbirth was a pioneering step and his sympathetic, tender and somewhat fatherly attitude toward the pregnant woman even overflowed into doctrinaire obstetrics.

The contributions of Lamaze and his disciples have further enriched the welfare of the parturient. By way of parenthesis, I should like to say that I met Dr. Lamaze at his Metal Workers' Hospital in Paris. He was a very large man, almost elephantine in appearance, yet seemed gentle and kind. Despite the language barrier, he took much time and great pains to tell me about his work. It is not my purpose to explain the theory or practice of psychoprophylaxis, for Mrs. Bing in her Six Practical Lessons For An Easier Childbirth has done this incredibly well, far better than could I or anyone else. I am not surprised that this is an exceptional book, for its author is an exceptional woman. Her sincere and personal interest in making childbirth a fulfilling and radiant experience for every woman illuminates each page.

I feel certain that these Six Lessons will become a bible for many young couples. How lucky they are to find it together, for if both study and follow its directions, their joint entrance into parenthood will almost certainly be a triumphant success. Having been a coworker of the author, I am especially pleased that her personality—rare spirituality and great humanity—comes through to the reader.

Alan F. Guttmacher, M.D.
died March 18, 1974
President, Planned Parenthood Federation
Formerly Chief of Obstetrics and Gynecology,
Mt. Sinai Hospital, New York City

Preface

This book begins where most books on childbirth and maternity end. Other teachers are content to romanticize the glorious aspects of childbearing, to acquaint you with the physiology of pregnancy, to explain fetal growth with beautiful pictures and to describe the mechanism of labor. Mrs. Bing's book, however, has a single aim: to teach you a method by which you can give birth by your own efforts.

Childbirth is one of the most stressful situations in human life. Childbirth demands an immense effort, comparable to the energy expended in a twelve-mile hike. Education that is limited to the physiology of pregnancy and the stages of labor can be compared to knowledge by map alone of a road on which you have to walk. Even if you know the map by heart, that information will not give you the physical training and stamina necessary to perform the hike. In labor, also, intellectual understanding is not enough. When you feel the oncoming uterine contraction—a totally new sensation—your first reaction may be to run away, to panic. Only the discipline imposed by an adequate training can prepare you to cope confidently and without apprehension with this task. You must learn to analyze the changing nature of the uterine contractions, adapt your body to these changes, and respond to them with appropriate breathing techniques.

Mrs. Bing can help you to do just this. But—a fair warning–it is not enough to understand the nature of these exercises; you must practice and practice until you can perform them automatically when you are in labor. Get your husband to coach you every evening until you are both letter-perfect in the method. Many hospitals today permit the husband to stay with his wife during the hours of labor and delivery.

Our technique is called the Lamaze Method, named after the famous obstetrician, Dr. Fernand Lamaze, who first introduced it in France in 1951. The technical name is the Psychoprophylactic Method of Childbirth, which means prevention or lessening of pain by psychological and physical means. The Lamaze Method does not believe in solitary mothers. You should be assisted and encouraged by the team surrounding you: the doctor, your husband, and the nurse.

By thoroughly mastering the method set forth in this book, you can participate actively in the birth of your baby—an experience you will never forget.

Heinz L. Luschinsky, M.D., F.A.C.O.G.

SIX PRACTICAL
LESSONS FOR AN
EASIER CHILDBIRTH

OUR CLASS
CONVENES

Women all over the world are preparing themselves for childbirth in a new and constructive way. They're learning about the changes that occur in the body during the nine months of gestation; they are doing exercises to prepare their bodies for giving birth; they are practicing new techniques of breathing and relaxation, which will help them ease pain and discomfort during labor and delivery.

This new method of preparation is an intelligent woman's approach to the difficult emotional and physical task of giving birth. Many such women—and their partners—are now taking classes similar to those presented here, but this book will allow prospective parents to prepare for childbirth at home, without any formal curriculum. Our book may be used as a supplement and guide to classes, but its primary value should be as a complete and thorough home course.

To make things as simple and useful as possible, let us begin together as if you were all attending the classes I have given thousands of parents-to-be. If you follow the course closely, practicing the exercises and using the techniques prescribed, I am sure you will have an active, happy and rewarding experience together.

AN INTRODUCTION
TO THE LESSONS

You are one of a group of five young couples arriving at my studio for your first lesson. The young women have various occupations: One is a dancer, on leave from a Broadway show; another is a secretary in a law office; the third is a schoolteacher; and there are two housewives, one of whom already has a little boy. The men's professions are varied: a lawyer, a book salesman, a broker, a mechanic, and a graduate student. All that these people have in common is their youth and the fact that each of them will be the parent of a new baby within the next two months.

We have found that the best time to start our course is toward the end of the seventh or the beginning of the eighth month, when a woman is psychologically ready to train herself for labor and delivery. She is beginning to feel the weight of her baby; she may have backaches; her abdominal muscles may feel weak. At this point she is more likely to accept and welcome the idea of training herself for the task ahead. If she had started too early in her pregnancy, the will to work hard at her exercises would very likely have diminished as the months wore on. Intensive training during the last phases of pregnancy not only provides the best physical preparation, but keeps methods and techniques fresh in the mind as actual labor and delivery arrive.

None of us in our class has met the others before, so there is a certain feeling of nervous anticipation in the air. I see that perhaps some of the men are a bit self-conscious— understandably. Without further delay I face the class and begin.

I introduce myself and present the couples to each other.

"Now," I continue, "I would like to ask each of you why you are here tonight and what you expect from these classes. Would each of you, both husband and wife, tell me your reasons for enrolling?"

The women respond first:

"I want to know exactly what will happen to me and to my baby during labor and delivery."

"I would like to have as little medication as possible. My physician suggested that if I want to help during labor and delivery, if I want to be awake and partici-

3

pate in the birth of my child, then I should attend this course."

"My husband and I want to participate in the birth of our child. A friend of ours attended your classes and told us what wonderful preparation they are."

"I was totally unprepared for the birth of my first child. It was a dreadful experience. This time I want to know what's going on and help myself as well as I can. And I'd like my husband to be with me when I give birth."

And from the men:

"I want to help my wife prepare for childbirth and be with her during labor and delivery."

"My wife's first childbirth was a harrowing experience for both of us. This time I want her to be prepared to help the doctor during labor and have a more pleasant and positive experience. We've heard that this course can do just that."

"Our doctor has said that the exercises, information and respiratory techniques we can learn here are the best possible training and preparation for childbirth."

"Susan asked me to come along tonight. I really don't know what I am supposed to do here. If it were I who had to have the baby, I'd certainly ask the doctor to take care of me and put me to sleep for it. . . ."

"This is an experience we want to share together."

Now we are no longer strangers to each other. We are all here together for the same purpose: to learn about the fabulous engineering feat of giving birth; to gain confidence, a sense of joyous anticipation, a thorough knowledge of how to handle the emotional and physical difficulties—not passively, helpless and unconscious or pacing the hall outside, but as active participants.

WHAT IS PSYCHOPROPHYLACTIC CHILDBIRTH?

Expectant mothers all over the world are preparing in exactly the same way for a conscious, healthy and happy experience. Our technique of preparation is called the psychoprophylactic method of childbirth, or the Lamaze technique. I think you should all know a little about how this technique began and how it spread so rapidly throughout the world.

The late Grantly Dick-Read originated the idea that pain during labor was caused primarily by fear. He wrote in his famous book, *Childbirth Without Fear,* that pain in childbirth could be greatly reduced or even totally eliminated through understanding the process of labor and delivery and through learning to relax properly. Dick-Read felt childbirth is essentially a "normal and physiologic process," and that any pain felt is present because of poor conditioning, the influence of Biblical stories, popular misconceptions, rumors and old wives' tales. Much of this concept has been generally accepted as valid, but we know now that all the education and "cultural conditioning" in the world cannot always provide a childbirth without any pain or discomfort whatsoever.

Dr. Dick-Read called his method "natural childbirth." Unfortunately, over the years the truth in this term has been almost totally obscured by layer upon layer of mysticism. It is thought to be a primitive childbirth, a childbirth completely without help or medication, a kind of endurance test. Dr. Dick-Read's pioneering work was—to a great extent—distorted, and the medical profession, as a result, has become wary of the term and concept of "natural childbirth."

This book presents a series of practical lessons in

what we term the psychoprophylactic, or Lamaze, method of childbirth. This method is not a technique of so-called "natural childbirth." On the contrary, it is a technique which is not at all natural, but acquired through concentrated effort and hard work on the part of the expectant mother and her husband. It is a method which provides an analgesic (or lessening of pain) achieved by physical means instead of by drugs or chemical means.

The psychoprophylactic technique originated in Russia, where it was first observed by the late Dr. Fernand Lamaze in 1951. Dr. Lamaze introduced the method to France and other European countries as well as China, Australia, Cuba and South America. In 1959 Marjorie Karmel published her book *Thank You, Dr. Lamaze* here in the United States. It was enormously influential in interesting American physicians and their patients in this new technique. I recommend that each of you read it if you have not already done so.

In 1959 the American Society for Psychoprophylaxis in Obstetrics, Inc., was established. Numerous chapters and affiliates have been formed all over the United States. Now more and more American women and their husbands are preparing for an educated childbirth. American doctors are urging many of their expectant mothers to prepare with this method, and American hospitals are gradually adapting their procedures to allow the active participation of husband and wife in labor and delivery.

What is the theory of the psychoprophylactic method? What does the term psychoprophylaxis mean? It simply means a psychological and physical preparation for childbirth, but you will come to understand it more completely as we work through each lesson together.

HOW DO WE CONTROL PAIN?

Many interesting studies have been made of the nature of pain. We have discovered, for example, that no matter what part of the body provides the source of pain—your foot, knee, abdomen or head—all pain is registered in the cerebral cortex, a part of the brain. It has also been determined that it is not possible to measure the actual *degree* of pain, although its effects, such as changes in blood content, hormonal output, respiration, etc., can be registered.

Experiments have shown that the perception of pain depends on many things that may occur simultaneously with the pain itself. The fact is that we can usually concentrate only on one thing at a time. While we concentrate on one object or sensation, other feelings become peripheral. I'm sure all of you have experiences every day which demonstrate this fact. Let's think of a few examples.

We all know that it is possible to become so engrossed in reading a good book on a train, a subway, or even in a room full of noisy people, that any kind of potential distractions—conversation, whistles, clanging of doors—cannot interrupt our intense concentration. We often hardly notice what is happening around us. We notice the same phenomenon with something that is actually happening within us. Suppose, with a bad headache, you go to the movies and see a really fine film. You may not notice the headache at all while you are watching the picture, but when the film ends, it strikes you with renewed force. What has happened? Simply that your concentration on the film was strong enough to eliminate the perception of pain. When you ceased concentrating, the headache again became the center of your attention.

Another sure way to increase the perception of pain is to overanticipate it. All I have to do is sit down in my dentist's chair and I immediately feel apprehensive and tense. When the dentist asks me to open my mouth so he can look at my teeth I begin to feel pain.

I think most women approach childbirth the same way. They anticipate nothing but pain. "Surely it must hurt. Why are there so many different medications for childbirth if it is not excruciatingly painful?" they ask themselves. And by anticipating and concentrating entirely on the sensation of pain, they leave themselves wide open for real suffering.

No one knows how painful labor actually is. We agree with Dr. Dick-Read that much of the pain in childbirth comes of anxiety and fear, but we do not think that education and "deconditioning" can eliminate it all. We believe that understanding the process of labor and childbirth can alleviate any unnecessary apprehension, and with it *unnecessary* pain. We believe that certain easy exercises can also help prepare the body for a more comfortable labor and delivery. But after all this understanding, education and physical preparation, there is still an undeniable discomfort during childbirth. Our task now is to attack and deal with this residual pain.

Now, if pain in labor were as mild as a headache, I am sure the problem could be solved by installing television sets in every labor room and allowing each expectant mother to watch a fascinating program during delivery. As you can imagine, this technique does not work, but there is nothing wrong with the idea behind it. Our goal throughout these lessons—in addition to understanding what happens during childbirth and learning various exercises to prepare our bodies—will be to recondition ourselves and to create a new center of concentration, thereby causing the awareness of pain to become peripheral. We have found that this is possible not just by looking at an outside object, but by concentrating on a very special activity of our own.

This special activity consists of active and difficult techniques of breathing, which will demand a great amount of concentrated effort. We use different breathing techniques because our breathing is so closely connected with all our activities, whether physical or emotional. Our respiration always automatically synchronizes itself with our activity. When we are asleep, our breathing is very slow. Sitting still, our breathing is also quite slow, but faster than when we are sleeping. When we walk, run, or climb stairs, our breathing changes in rate and intensity. The same changes occur emotionally. Our breathing is slow if we are calm. It speeds up when we are excited or disturbed.

You will learn to change your breathing deliberately during labor, adjusting it to the changing characteristics of the uterine contractions. This will demand an enormous concentrated effort on your part. Not a concentration on pain, but a concentration on your own activity in synchronizing your respiration to the signals that you receive from the uterus. This strenuous activity will create a new center of concentration in the brain, thereby causing the painful sensations during labor to become peripheral, to reduce their intensity. And at the same time, you will learn to relax your body in such a way that you will allow the uterus to work under optimum conditions.

These then are the basic principles of our psychoprophylactic technique of childbirth: education, understanding, preliminary exercises and a technique of special breathing activity and relaxation during labor. I will give you these precision tools to work with. It will be up to you to take these tools and use them as your need demands.

HOW WELL DOES IT WORK?

We are often asked to give statistics about our method. Many physicians want to know whether birth injuries, prematurity, hemorrhaging, etc. can be reduced by using our method. Studies made in France and many other countries show that the psychoprophylactic method does reduce these complications. But there is one important factor that cannot be measured statistically. That is: How does a rewarding experience in childbirth enhance a young couple's relationship with each other? How does the feeling of achievement, of having collaborated in the performance of a difficult job, such as giving birth, affect the husband and wife who have worked hard together toward this goal?

As I have already mentioned, the partner's role is crucial. He must help his wife while she is learning the respiratory techniques. He must see that she is properly relaxed during both practice and actual childbirth. He must help her concentrate on her breathing and signal the length of time between contractions. He must be constantly ready to provide both moral and physical support, not only by his own emotional and physical involvement, but also by the application of specific techniques that we will learn here in class. This can surely be the most joyous and satisfying experience a man and woman can have together.

We women do not give birth very often during our lives. In fact, in our country at this specific period of time, most babies that are born are born by choice and not by chance. This is a very new development, and I'm sure a sociologically and psychologically significant one. I would like to dream and think that a country whose citizens were all desired, might make a wonderful future place for our children to live in. It would be a shame if this great event were to be a traumatic experience, one to be put out of our minds rather than happily remembered. I want to help you make the experience of childbirth a rewarding one which you can perform with dignity and joy, and which you and your husband can share together in happy collaboration.

I don't want to make amateur obstetricians out of you. I am sure you have all chosen your doctor or midwife carefully, and that you respect his or her judgment. But I want you to realize that giving birth is really a team effort. The team consists of you and your husband, myself as the teacher, and of course the nurses and your physician. We all have our roles to play.

This brings me to another important point I want to make before we begin our first lesson. I have often been asked the number of successes and failures among my students. I want you to realize that I do not accept the concept of failure in regard to the women I prepare for childbirth. Before we train in our method, we all start off at a point I call minus zero. Every one of you will achieve zero plus, and this will be your point of total success. There is no absolute goal, no threshold that all or any of us must reach. You certainly must not feel any kind of guilt or sense of failure if you require some medication, or if you experience discomfort. This is a completely individual thing, depending on the physical nature of your body and its proportions, the size and shape of your baby, and many other factors.

If for any reason medical complications should arise, it is no longer up to you to handle them. Such problems are completely out of your hands, and any decisions of a medical nature lie with your physician. And let us keep in mind that in case mechanical difficulties do occur, your training and active cooperation can frequently help to avoid the use of instruments, or even the necessity of a Caesarean section. Your conscious help and participation can provide invaluable assistance to your physician. You and your doctor will continue to function as a team.

And finally, I think that both of you should visit your doctor together for prenatal examinations. You as women are not having the baby alone. There are two of you creating a family. From the shared beginning through your pregnancy, you are involved together, learning not only to give birth, but how to parent.

LESSON 1

How your body changes during pregnancy;
the importance of good posture;
the three stages of labor: contractions,
delivery of baby, expulsion of placenta

Let's begin this lesson by looking at some pictures (on the following pages) to help you understand the changes that occur in your body during pregnancy.

BODY CHANGES
DURING PREGNANCY

Our first drawing represents the non-pregnant woman. Notice the shape of the uterus. Pay particular attention to the bottleneck opening, which is called the cervix. You can also see the close proximity of the uterus to the bladder, the intestines filling the abdomen, the stomach immediately under the diaphragm, and directly above that, the diaphragm and lungs.

The second drawing shows a pregnant woman, the fetus here about five months old. The uterus is really an extremely elastic, muscular bag. As the baby grows, the uterus expands, moving out of the pelvic cavity into the abdominal cavity, thereby pushing the intestines up and back.

In the third drawing, the fetus is in the ninth month. The uterus now fills the entire abdomen, while the intestines are pushed further up against the stomach and diaphragm, compressing the lungs to a certain degree. This will explain why you are short of breath, why you may occasionally experience heartburn and why your stomach often feels uncomfortable after eating. You can also see how the pressure of the uterus against your bladder is causing all those frequent trips to the bathroom.

Take a closer look at the cervix in drawing number 3. You will observe a small plug at the bottleneck

---

14

opening. This plug consists of mucus and tiny blood vessels. It prevents bacteria from entering the cervix and causing infection during pregnancy. This plug of mucus is a safety device, and should be reassuring to you. Its presence allows activities such as intercourse, swimming, taking a bath. All these things are considered perfectly safe, unless of course your physician has given you specific instructions to avoid such activities during your pregnancy. Making love during pregnancy is generally considered safe. Perhaps the desire in the woman or in the man may vary in the three trimesters. Obviously you will have to be more inventive and find new positions for intercourse and pleasuring. But don't be afraid to make love. It's virtually impossible to hurt the baby.

As her self-image may suffer somewhat when a woman's figure changes in pregnancy, she may need a great deal of reassurance that she is still desirable. And I can't think of a more delightful way of being reassured than by being loved and making love.

Look at the fourth drawing very carefully. You will notice that the cervix has become shorter, permitting your intestines and stomach more room. The pressure on the bladder has increased. Towards the end of your pregnancy the baby is likely to drop, settling into the pelvic cavity. This is not a sudden drop, but gradual. At this point, you will notice that, although you can breathe more easily, there is increased pressure on your bladder and thighs.

Perhaps well-meaning people will tell you how "low" you carry, and overwhelm you with tales of what this might mean. Take no notice of their well-meant advice, but rather ask your doctor if you are in doubt about any symptom or discomfort. Your doctor will tell you now that the head of your baby has become "engaged." What does this mean? It's really quite simple: the head has entered the pelvis, a cavity composed of the sacrum, the iliac bone, and the symphysis pubis. The engagement of the baby's head is an encouraging sign.

1

Lungs

Diaphragm

Stomach

Intestines

Uterus

Bladder

Symphysis pubis

Urethra

Spine

Rectum

Cervix

Vagina

Anus

2

1. This illustration shows the position of
the uterus in a non-pregnant woman
and its relation to the other organs

2. At five months the baby has entered
the abdominal cavity, exerting some pressure
against the diaphragm and lungs

3. In ninth month the baby fills nearly
the entire abdomen but nonetheless internal
organs continue to function well

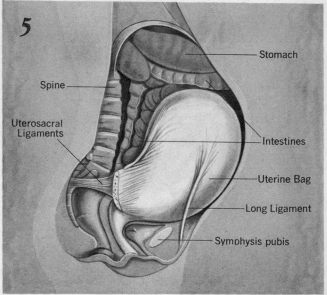

Stomach

Spine

Uterosacral
Ligaments

Intestines

Uterine Bag

Long Ligament

Symphysis pubis

4. At the end of the ninth month the baby's head has become engaged, wedged now between pubic bone and sacrum

5. This shows the baby as it is contained in the uterine bag, which is supported by ligaments at the sides and the back

You now know that you are getting closer to labor. This may happen as long as three weeks before your due date, or it may happen only a few days before you go into labor. Occasionally the head will engage only when you are already in labor.

The fifth drawing shows the entire uterine bag. This bag is supported by ligaments, which act like columns supporting a building. There are two long ligaments, one on each side, and two short ones attached to the lower part of your spine. You may occasionally feel a sharp pain in your groin when you stretch suddenly, cough or sneeze. This picture shows you that such an occasional sudden pain is caused by stretching the long ligaments. The pain is of no consequence, and I hope you will be better able to put up with this occasional discomfort now that you realize what causes it.

IMPORTANCE
OF GOOD POSTURE

The ligaments attached to your lower spine may cause backache during pregnancy. Backache in pregnancy is a frequent occurrence. Unfortunately we often increase the normal strain on our back by poor posture. It is so easy for us to take the line of least resistance when carrying a heavy baby. By letting the abdomen hang and leaning back slightly we weaken our abdominal muscles, simply by not using them. We may also strain the back muscles by overextending them. It is of the utmost importance that we learn to use our bodies correctly during pregnancy.

When standing we must always remember that the crown of our head is the highest part of the body. If you raise your head as indicated in the next pictures you find that the rest of your body aligns itself. There is no need to tuck in your bottom or your abdominal muscles. This will naturally occur if you thus raise your head.

You will find that good posture will enable you to walk more gracefully, putting far less strain on your abdominal and back muscles. And believe it or not, you will find that good posture will ease the pressure on your bladder. I suggest that your husband remind you now and then to "stretch up."

Good posture will also prevent fatigue. It is normal for you to tire more easily when you are pregnant, but don't let your tiredness accumulate. Rest during the day, if only for ten minutes at a time. Sit down, or better still, lie down with your legs raised. You will soon feel your energy coming back and be able to get through a long day with greater ease.

Here is another exercise which will help you to strengthen the pelvic floor, make it more elastic, and make you more aware of your pelvic floor muscles, which you'll have to relax when you have to push your baby out. The exercise is called the "Kegel exercise," after the late Dr. Kegel, who described and used the exercise in the treatment of incontinence and poor pelvic muscle tone.

I will teach you now to exercise your pubio-coccygeal muscle, which is the muscle band leading from near the pubic bone to near the coccyx. This muscle is shaped like a figure of eight, it surrounds your sphincters and passages, and its most important function is to support the bladder, the vagina and uterus, and the rectum.

Sit comfortably, legs slightly apart; lean forward a

little. Now tighten your front passage as if to stop yourself from urinating. Then squeeze your vagina, and finally tighten your back passage as if you were preventing a bowel movement. Hold it—one—two—three —four—five—six—and release. Think "release" and you will find that you can relax even more. Always connect your body movements with your mind. If you think the movement, you will find that you can perform the exercise much more thoroughly.

Repeat this Kegel exercise at least 20–30 times a day. You can do it in a standing, sitting or lying position; while driving your car, in the subway or bus, at boring parties or during TV commercials. Nobody will ever notice you are doing it. However, you will soon notice that you are carrying your baby better, there will be less pressure on your thighs, and as a special bonus, you and your partner will find that love making is even more fun when you have the ability to contract and relax your vaginal muscles easily.

Exercising your pelvic floor muscles will improve the muscle tone and increase the elasticity of your perineum—the area between the anus and the vulva—so that it will stretch easily when your baby descends. Frequent use of these muscles will also make you conscious of their position and function, and will enable you to help the smooth expulsion of your baby through conscious neuromuscular control, just as the "concentration-relaxation" exercises trained you to develop relaxation and control over your arms, legs and facial muscles.

Practice this exercise diligently from now until you give birth. It is also one of the most important exercises to do shortly *after* you've given birth. Once you have delivered the baby and are back in your room, start contracting your pelvic floor. Or even on the delivery table. You will probably feel sore and numb in your pelvic area. The stitches from your episiotomy may feel irritated. You may be afraid to urinate or have a bowel movement. By using your Kegel exercises there

*Gail demonstrates a very poor posture—
one that will give her a backache and will
weaken her abdominal muscles*

and then, you can speed up the healing process of the
episiotomy and begin a much more comfortable post-
partum (after delivery) period.

I would like every woman to practice this pelvic-
floor exercise for the rest of her life in order to retain
good muscle tone. This may prevent weakness or even
a prolapse in later life.

Now let us look at the following pictures so that we
may see the actual process of labor. In the illustration
on page 26 you see a baby ready to be born. The mother
is lying on her back. You will recognize the spine, the

*Lifting the top of the head correctly aligns
the body, supports the baby and helps
reduce pressure on the bladder*

anus, the vagina, the urinary opening or urethra, the
uterus with its bottleneck cervix (which in this picture
has lost its plug) and of course the baby, which is facing the mother's hip.

THE FIRST
STAGE OF LABOR

Labor is divided into three stages. During the first
stage, the uterus begins to contract involuntarily—that

is, entirely on its own—thereby pulling on the cervix. The cervix becomes soft, thins out and flattens. This is called the *effacement* of the cervix. In the majority of women, the effacement starts towards the end of pregnancy, as early as two to three weeks before the birth of the baby. You may have already felt an occasional tightening in your abdomen. These tightenings are contractions of the uterus and are entirely painless. These preliminary contractions are called Braxton-Hicks contractions. They are named after an Englishman, Mr. Braxton-Hicks, who was the first to describe them in medical literature. Once labor proper begins, you will feel the uterine contractions more distinctly. These new, stronger contractions will cause the cervix to dilate.

The opening of the cervix can be compared to the neck of a very tight turtleneck sweater. Imagine yourself trying to put the sweater on: You pull it and stretch it until you have finally opened it far enough for you to push your head through. Thus the uterus has to pull on the cervix and stretch it with each contraction until it has opened to the widest diameter of the baby's head. Only then can you start to push your baby out. We say that the first stage of labor has ended when the cervix has opened fully to "5 fingers" or "10 centimeters."

I would like you to remember both these terms for the dilation of the cervix. Your doctor will examine you internally during labor and let you know how far along you are in precisely this language. He'll say you are "3 fingers" or "7 centimeters" open. I feel that communication between you and your physician is of the utmost importance before and during your labor. It is therefore essential for you to be acquainted with this terminology. Thus you can be fully aware of all the signposts on your road through labor to delivery.

THE SECOND
STAGE OF LABOR

The door is now open. The second stage of labor is the expulsion of the baby. The uterus now works like a piston expelling the baby. Your lungs, diaphragm and strong abdominal muscles will provide the necessary power for this piston. You will see, in the picture on page 28, that the baby has rotated now and that the symphysis pubis acts as a pivotal point or fulcrum for the baby. The baby now faces the mother's spine and its head is at an angle. As the head gradually pushes through the vagina or birth canal the crown appears at the vulva or outlet of the vagina. At this point the doctor will talk of the "crowning" of the baby's head. The head now emerges, and you will see from the next illustrations that it is being rotated once again (this time externally, with the help of the doctor), to aid the expulsion of the shoulders. Once the shoulders have been delivered, the rest of the baby's body will slip out easily. The birth of the baby is the end of the second stage of labor.

A moment before you deliver the baby's head your doctor may make a small incision, called the "episiotomy," in the mouth of the vagina. This minor surgical procedure is performed to avoid possible tearing of your tissue as the baby's head is delivered. Your physician will decide whether or not an episiotomy is necessary. It is quite commonly done in America, since a small, neat incision can be easily repaired, and heals quickly. A tear with a ragged edge may create difficulties. The incision is frequently done with a local anesthetic.

It is important for you to realize that an episiotomy does not in any way interfere with your desire and ability to use the psychoprophylactic method of childbirth. In fact it is good to remember once again that

1

Symphysis pubis

Vagina

Bladder

Urethra

Placenta

Spine   Bag of Waters   Rectum   Cervix   Anus

2

1. This baby is ready to be born: the mother is lying on her back, her baby facing her right hip; the cervix is still thick and long; preliminary contractions have not yet occurred

2. Here begins the first stage of labor: contractions have started; the baby has begun to move down and the cervix becomes shorter and flatter in the process called effacement

3. Baby rotates slightly as contractions during the first stage of labor continue. The cervix dilates; here it has opened about halfway, which is termed 2½ fingers or 5 centimeters

4. At the end of the first stage of labor, cervix is fully dilated (5 fingers or 10 centimeters); the baby's head is entering the stretched vagina and putting pressure upon the rectum

5. During second stage of labor, the baby faces the mother's spine, flexing and extending its soft head to pivot around the pubic bone as it is pushed on through the birth canal

6. The head rotates once again on delivery to allow the shoulders and arms to emerge; the rest of the body slips out easily; expulsion is completed and the baby is born

your labor and delivery will involve teamwork between you and your husband and between you and your physician. The performance or nonperformance of an episiotomy will be entirely your doctor's responsibility, though you should discuss your ideas and feelings about this process with your doctor, and you should know what you can do to acquire good control of your pelvic floor muscles to help yourself and the doctor. Don't forget to practice these exercises at least 20–30 times a day.

THE THIRD STAGE OF LABOR

The third stage of labor is the expulsion of the afterbirth or "placenta." Once the baby has been born, the doctor will clamp and cut the umbilical cord. This procedure does not hurt either you or your baby. A few minutes after the birth of your child your uterus will contract again and your doctor will ask you to push once more to expel the placenta. He will generally help you by exerting pressure on your abdomen. The expulsion of the placenta is generally very fast, taking only a few minutes.

This has been our first class. For the next session I would like you to wear shorts, tights, slacks or any comfortable garment that will allow you to perform our exercises easily. We will continue to look at these pictures and discuss the process of labor in more detail. I will never teach an exercise by itself, but will always explain—with the help of these pictures—why we perform certain exercises during each phase of labor.

LESSON 2

Learning to relax and conserve your
energy through neuromuscular control
exercises; simple but basic exercises
to prepare your body for childbirth

This lesson will be a more active one for you and your husband. We are going to do exercises today, which I divide into two groups:

1. Neuromuscular control exercises, which I also call Concentration-Relaxation exercises.

2. Body-building or limbering-up, exercises.

One of the primary aims during labor must be the conservation of energy. You should never exert more energy than is actually needed for efficient performance during this period. By conserving energy you will avoid unnecessary fatigue. If you are tense, if you thrash around or dig your fingernails into the mattress (or your partner's arm), you are wasting energy.

NEUROMUSCULAR CONTROL EXERCISES

Neuromuscular control exercises are extremely important. You must remember that the uterus will be working hard during labor. That part of your body will be extremely active. Your task will be to allow it to work freely while you keep the rest of your body deliberately relaxed. These exercises will help you to develop muscle control, to isolate muscle groups, and at the same time make you aware of which muscle groups are in use and which are at rest.

These exercises will have to be practiced with your partner. Not only is it impossible for you to check on your own relaxation, but I want your partner to give the commands, which I will demonstrate. I also want him to check on your tension and relaxation. In this way you will learn to react to your partner's signals instantly, and he will learn to recognize any tensions in your body. You will be involved in labor and may not notice that while trying to control the uterine contractions, you have tensed your legs or arms or face. Your partner, however, will see these tensions immediately, and you will be able to cooperate and relax whenever he gives the signal. I think the great advantage of your working together is that since you have shared your lives for some time, you know each other very well, and are therefore much more aware of each other's tensions and difficulties than a strange nurse or doctor could ever be. And this intimate knowledge can be used in working together in labor and correcting tensions. I am often sure that I can tell what kind of day my husband has had when he comes home, even before he has said a word. It's his facial expression, perhaps, or the way he holds his shoulders. I'm not even sure what it is. Try it sometime with your partner. Watch him or her, and soon you'll be able to spot tensions and weak points. This will make it easier to react to each other's signals.

This will require considerable discipline from both of you. Your partner's commands have to be as disciplined as your reaction. By developing this kind of teamwork, it will be easy for you to react to his signals, even under stress.

Lie on the floor, on your back, a pillow under your head and another pillow or bolster under your knees. Begin by taking a very deep and relaxing inhalation-exhalation. I call such a deep relaxing breath "a cleansing breath." From now on, when I speak of a "cleansing breath," you will know that I want you to take a deep breath, then exhale and relax your whole body. Your partner should now check your relaxation. Let him gently lift your arm by holding your wrist in his hand and feeling the whole weight of your arm and shoulder. Let your arm bend at the elbow so that every joint is relaxed. Once your partner feels the weight of your arm, he can then try to move your arm freely from side to side to check on your absolute relaxation. When he lets go of your arm, it should drop heavily to the floor. Let him try your other arm. To check the relaxation of your legs, your partner must place his hands under your knees and gently lift them a little off the pillow. Your heels should remain on the floor. If your leg is tense, he will not be able to bend your knee easily and he should therefore give the command, "Relax."

Once your partner is satisfied that you are relaxed, he should give the following command: "Contract your right arm." You will then tense your arm, shoulder, elbow, fist, and raise your arm, holding it straight before you a few inches off the floor. Your partner should check on the tension in your right arm, then check on the complete relaxation of your left arm and both legs —while you are still holding up your right arm. The next command is: "Release your arm," and your arm should fall absolutely relaxed to the floor.

Command: "Contract your left arm." Tense the arm, shoulder, elbow, fist, and raise your left arm, holding it straight before you, a few inches off the floor. Again your partner should check first on the tension in your left arm and then, while the left arm is tense, he must check on the relaxation of your right arm and both your legs. Next command: "Release your left arm."

Command: "Contract your right leg." Stiffen your thigh, hold the leg straight and flex your foot. You don't have to raise your leg. While you are holding your leg stiff, your partner should check first on the tension of the right leg, then on the relaxation of your left leg and both arms, checking your shoulders and face at the same time. Command: "Release your leg."

Command: "Contract right arm, right leg." Again your partner will check on your tension on the right side and your release of muscles on your left. "Release."

Command: "Contract left arm, left leg." Be sure to stiffen your leg well and to flex your foot in order to

1. Gail and Bill begin the neuromuscular control exercises. Note complete relaxation, good support under head, knees.

2. Bill commands: "Contract right arm", as Gail responds he checks carefully to make sure that her left arm is relaxed

3. While Gail's right arm is contracted,
Bill checks on the relaxation of her legs
by lifting her knees from the pillow

4. "Contract right arm and right leg."
Again Bill must make sure that both her
left arm and left leg remain relaxed

5. Now commands become more complex as Gail must contract her opposing arms and legs while Bill checks carefully

6. With diligent practice and Bill's cooperation, Gail learns to concentrate and relax in automatic response to command

7. *Gail relaxes in an alternate position: sitting.*
Bill checks the relaxation of her right arm

tense the calf muscles. Your partner will check your tension and relaxation. "Release."

Command: "Contract your right arm, left leg." Your partner will check and give the command: "Release."

Command: "Contract your left leg, arm, right leg." Your partner will check and release.

You will soon realize how very difficult it is to work with one part of your body while keeping the rest of your body relaxed. It will demand your absolute concentration and special attention. You will discover that only with continued and repeated practice will you be able to isolate muscle groups and automatically follow your partner's signals. You should practice these exercises at least once a day. Let me point out once again that the purpose of these exercises is to make you aware of your body, to establish a source of teamwork between you and your partner and to enable you to be economical with all energy expended during labor. If lying down is difficult for you, the exercise can be easily performed in a comfortable chair. You realize, of course, that you won't tense and lift an arm in labor, or tense a leg. This exercise is a training for labor, to make you become aware of your body and thus able to separate muscle groups, relaxing part of your body as other parts are working.

BODY-BUILDING EXERCISES

I think we all tend to slow down considerably during pregnancy, partly because of the added weight we have to carry, partly because of our own anxiety that we might somehow injure the baby when we stretch, bend or simply move around. So many people shower us with well-meant advice not to do this, that, or the other. I am sure you have been told by someone not to reach or raise your arms above your head, not to cross your legs, etc. If we really followed all this well-in tended counsel, we could hardly move at all.

It is perfectly safe to lead a normal life and to move about as much as you have always done, as long as it does not hurt and you don't get too tired. I always like to quote Dr. Alan Guttmacher here. He told us once that as a young obstetrician he used to forbid his patients to play tennis, though he allowed every other sport. In discussing this with a colleague, the colleague said, "Strange, I forbid my patients to do swimming and allow them to do anything else!" They realized that they were both discouraging the particular sport they themselves didn't like or were poor at.

The limbering-up exercises I will show you are meant to make you feel better *now*. They will strengthen your back and abdominal muscles so you can carry the additional weight of the baby with comparative

EXERCISE 1

*Bill and Gail assume a basic position, sitting
tailor-fashion; this helps to stretch the pelvis
and the muscles of the thigh*

ease. They will help you to spread your legs far apart,
which will be most useful for you when you have to
push out your baby. Some of the exercises will improve the tone of your pelvic-floor muscles.

For the following exercises you do not need a pillow
under your head or knees. And don't practice any of
these exercises on your bed, even if you think your
mattress is very hard. The hardest mattress is still too
soft. You need firm support. Use the floor, covered by a
rug or blanket.

Exercise 1: Sit cross-legged (tailor fashion) on the floor,
back relaxed and slightly rounded. Use this sitting position as much as possible from now on. It will help to
strengthen your pelvic-floor muscles and stretch your
thigh muscles. We rarely sit in this position any more,
with all our comfortable upholstered chairs and
couches. I suggest you do this in the evenings while

EXERCISE 2

To stretch her muscles more, Gail puts
the soles of her feet together and
exerts slight pressure upon her knees

Gail assumes an alternate position to
stretch her pelvis and her thighs

you read, sew, watch television or play chess with your husband. When you get tired of sitting like this, stretch your legs for a while, shake them out, then resume the position.

Exercise 2: Sit on the floor and put the soles of your feet together, then pull your feet as close to your body as possible. Put your hands on your thighs and press them gently down. You will feel the muscles pull on the inside of your thighs. For those of you who have very long ligaments, this exercise may be very easy. Your thighs will practically touch the floor with little effort. If so, try the following exercise: Sit on the floor, stretch your legs well apart and turn your knees out. Then lean your body forward, and you will feel a good pull in your thighs.

Exercise 3: Lie on your back, arms at your sides. Take a deep, cleansing breath. Now raise your right leg up slowly, pointing your toes, breathing in slowly through your nose. Be sure to keep both knees straight. Then flex your foot, lower your leg slowly to the ground and at the same time exhale through your mouth and lips. Repeat with your left leg. Take care to synchronize your breathing with the raising and lowering of your leg, to point your toes as you go up, and to flex your foot as you go down, keeping both legs straight at all times. Repeat this exercise five times for each leg.

Exercise 4: Lie on your back, stretching your arms at right angles from your body. Take a deep cleansing breath. Then raise your right leg, pointing your toes and inhaling through your nose. Follow this by flexing your foot, and lower your leg to the right side as far as is comfortable as you breathe out through your mouth. Then point your toes, inhale through your nose and raise your leg; flex your foot and lower your leg to the floor, as you breathe out through your mouth. Repeat this with the left leg. See to it that the hip opposite the moving leg remains flat on the floor. Work on this exercise so that you can do it at least three times with each leg.

EXERCISE 3

1. To begin this body-building exercise,
Gail and Bill lie flat on a hard floor with
no support, inhaling and exhaling deeply

2. As Gail and Bill inhale through their nose,
they raise their right legs slowly, keeping
their knees straight and toes pointed

3. Gail and Bill flex feet, exhale through their lips and lower legs slowly, synchronizing their breathing and their movements

4. The exercise is completed when Gail and Bill have raised each leg five times and take a deep inhalation-exhalation to relax

VARIATION
OF EXERCISE 3

1. Keep right leg bent, foot resting on
the door, inhaling and exhaling deeply

2. Stretch left leg up, pointing
the toes and inhaling comfortably

3. Flex foot and lower leg slowly as you exhale

4. The exercise is completed when each
leg has been raised five times and a deep
inhalation-exhalation taken to relax

EXERCISE 4

1. Keep right leg bent, foot resting on the floor, inhaling and exhaling deeply

2. While inhaling through nose, raise leg as high as you can, pointing your toes

3. At point of highest elevation flex your
foot and lower your leg slowly outward
toward the arm of the same side

4. To return to the original position first
point your toes, raise your leg up
again, and inhale through your nose

5. You must now flex your foot again;
exhale slowly through your mouth while
gradually lowering your leg to the floor

Exercise 5: This is my favorite. It strengthens the back as well as the abdominal muscles. It is a good exercise whether you are pregnant or not. Have your husband do it as well, particularly if he often feels tired or his back is bothering him.

Again lie on your back and bend your knees so that your feet are firmly on the ground. Press your entire back, including your shoulders, firmly against the floor, pulling in the lower abdominal muscles at the same time and letting your buttocks lift very slightly off the floor. Then release. This exercise should be done with controlled breathing. Start by breathing in, then exhale through your mouth slowly and, as you exhale, press your back against the floor, contracting your abdominal muscles. Breathe in as you release your back and abdomen. You will find that you can flatten your back

EXERCISE 5

1. Barbara does the important back exercise on the floor with bent knees, inhaling slowly and keeping her back relaxed

2. Now she exhales slowly, flattens her shoulders and back against the hard floor, contracts her abdominal muscles, while Tom checks that she flattens her back completely against the floor

EXERCISE 6

1. Lie on your back, knees and feet
separated, feet firmly on the ground

2. Raise your buttocks off the floor, hips
raised toward the ceiling, as you breathe in

*3. Lower your back slowly, vertebra
by vertebra, as you exhale*

much more effectively if you exhale when doing it. Be
sure to use correct breathing techniques: exhale when
you flatten yourself: inhale when you release your back.
Exercise 6: Lie on your back and bend your knees, feet
firmly on the ground. This time, separate your feet and
bring your heels as close to your buttocks as possible.
Now breathe in and raise your buttocks and back off
the floor—push your hips toward the ceiling. Then as
you exhale slowly, lower your back, vertebra by vertebra, like a "string of pearls," bit by bit. Keep your
hips up till the end, then slowly lower them and rest.
Repeat this exercise three times.
Exercise 7: Sit cross-legged and stretch your arms up
high. Look at your fingertips and pull yourself out of
your ribs. If you really look at your fingertips, you can
stretch another half-inch. Now relax.

EXERCISE 7

1. *Felice, Barbara and Gail stretch spinal columns, looking up at their finger-tips*

We will start with our third group of exercises, respiration exercises, in the next lesson. Be sure to practice daily with your partner, so that he can supervise and correct you, and so that both of you can understand the purpose of our first two groups of exercises.

1. During pregnancy, be sure to rise
from a lying position in a manner that
will not strain your abdominal muscles

2. From the lying position, first bend your
legs and knees up, still supporting
yourself with both hands at your sides

3. Keeping your legs parallel, roll over to one side so that your weight rests on one hip, supported by both hands

4. Now you can push yourself with both hands to a sitting position from which it will be easy for you to stand up

LESSON 3

Three phases of uterine contractions:
latent, accelerated, transitional;
our first breathing technique; partner's
role during practice at home

It is always important to review the material covered in our previous lesson. These reviews are an essential aspect of your training. Not that I don't trust you to practice diligently, but it is imperative to see how proficient you have become, and to correct a few things that you may have misunderstood. Therefore bear with me when I encourage you to repeat and repeat the exercises. This is the discipline of the Lamaze technique. You will have to learn to channel your energy correctly for your labor, and I will help you do so.

Let us review the neuromuscular control exercises. Do you remember what these are for? Do we actually tense one arm or leg in labor? Certainly not. These exercises will teach you to relax part of your body while the rest is working, and they will also help to establish teamwork between you and your partner. Lie comfortably on the floor, a pillow under your head, a bolster under your knees. Take a deep "cleansing breath" and relax. Let your partner check your relaxation before he gives the commands.

Then: Contract right arm. Release. Contract left arm (partner should check thoroughly). Release. Contract right arm and right leg (partner checks). Release. Contract left arm and left leg (partner checks). Release. Contract right arm and left leg (partner checks). Release. Contract left arm and right leg (partner checks). Release.

I hope you will notice how much you have improved in one week. It should be much easier for you to isolate muscle groups and to follow your partner's commands. Some of you will learn faster than others, but in a relatively short time you will have learned this difficult body control. Remember also that it is really a good idea to have this control whether you are pregnant or not.

Now let us review the body-building exercises. These can be done without your partner's help. Take the pillows away and sit on the floor cross-legged. Then put the soles of your feet together, your hands on your thighs, and press your thighs gently down.

Next lie on your back, arms at your sides. Take a deep cleansing breath. Raise your right leg slowly, pointing your toes. Breathe in slowly through your nose as you raise your leg. Flex your foot, lower your leg, keep your knee straight, and breathe out slowly through your mouth. Repeat with your left leg. Repeat this exercise five times for each leg, or the variation to this exercise (p. 45).

Lie on your back on the floor. Extend your arms at right angles to your sides. Inhale and exhale deeply. Bend left leg. While inhaling through your nose, raise right leg up as far as you can, pointing your toes, keeping your knee straight. Then lower your leg gently to the right as far as is comfortable, flexing your foot and exhaling through your mouth. Then inhaling again, raise your leg to upright position, while pointing your toes. Finally, exhale slowly and lower your leg again to its original position, flexing your foot. Inhale and exhale deeply. Repeat this series with your left leg. Do this exercise at least three times with each leg.

Lie on your back, bend your knees and keep your feet firmly on the floor. Press your back hard against the floor, straightening it right to your shoulders, tightening your lower abdominal muscles at the same time. Then release your back. Do not forget to exhale when you flatten your back, and inhale when you release your back.

Lie on your back, bend your knees, feet firmly on the floor, heels close to your buttocks. Inhale and slowly raise your back off the floor, hips against the ceiling, then exhale slowly as you lower your back vertebra by vertebra and rest your back.

Here is the last exercise: the spinal stretch. Sit cross-legged, bend your arms to your shoulders, then stretch them well into the air. Look at your fingertips, stretch a little more, and a little more, and a little more. Then relax and breathe deeply. You will find it feels wonderful to be able to stretch, and you can rest assured that it will not do you or the baby any harm whatsoever.

If any of you have been to physical fitness or dance classes, you will probably be able to think of other suitable exercises. Be sure, however, never to raise or lower both legs at the same time when you are lying flat on your back.

THE THREE PHASES OF THE FIRST STAGE OF LABOR

I want you to look once again at the pictures and drawings showing the first stage of labor. You will remember that the first stage of labor consists of the effacement—or thinning out and flattening—of the cervix, and its dilation to 5 fingers or 10 centimeters.

We divide the first stage of labor into three parts or phases.

Part One is the *latent* or *preliminary* phase of labor, during which the cervix effaces fully and dilates to about 1½ fingers or 3 centimeters.

Part Two is the dilation of the cervix from about 1½ fingers or 3 centimeters to approximately 4 fingers or 8 centimeters. This phase is called the *accelerated*, or active phase of labor.

Part Three is the dilation of the cervix from 4 fingers to full dilation or 5 fingers or, in centimeters, from 8 to 10. This phase is called the *transition* phase.

The uterine contractions change their character in the three phases of the first stage of labor. The uterus, like any other muscle in our body, contracts and relaxes. This is the nature of muscle. Stretch your arm out, then bend it slowly. In doing this, you have used a muscle—that is, you have contracted the biceps.

When you straighten your arm again you release the tension in the biceps. Suppose you were to draw a diagram of a muscular contraction, it would look like a curve, or a wave pattern.

Look at the diagrams on page 62, which will show you the changes in the waves that occur during the three phases of the first stage of labor. I like to compare these waves to those at the oceanside. There are many people, and you may be among them, who can surf-ride very well, meeting each wave with confidence and riding with it and through it. And then there are people like myself: I don't know how to cope with these waves. Should I face them? Should my back be turned towards them? And before I have managed to make up my mind, the wave has hit me, thrown me over. I scrape my knees, get water in my mouth and nose and scramble out exhausted, telling myself not to try again until the next summer.

I think one can compare the trained or untrained woman in labor to the person who has learned or who has not learned to ride the waves at the beach.

A few years ago, though, a friend showed me how to manage the waves when we were swimming together, and though I never became an expert at it, I could manage to ride, if not most, at least many of the waves—and I felt very good about it. Even if I missed one, I was confident that I could cope with the next one. And so it is in labor: you probably won't catch every wave; you'll goof occasionally, but you will stay on top of most of them, and you will say as one of my students said, "it actually got easier and easier the more labor progressed, because I got better and better." Another of my students told me, "The fact that I could participate in the birth of my child and knew what to do and actively give birth, was the greatest ego trip I've ever had in my life!"

In the *preliminary* or *latent phase* of labor (1) the waves are gentle and shallow. One wave may last from 30 to 60 seconds, and the intervals of rest may vary

3 PHASES OF
FIRST STAGE OF LABOR

During this early phase of labor, contractions occur in the form of mild waves that come at irregular intervals

The accelerated phase is the longest and most active period of labor. Waves become higher and last longer

This phase is the most intense and the shortest phase of the first stage of labor. Waves are erratic and sharp

BREATHING EXERCISES FOR FIRST STAGE OF LABOR

1

Preliminary Phase   30-60 Second Contractions

1 minute → | 1 minute → | 1 minute →

5-20 minute intervals between contractions

BREATHING

CONTRACTION

Begin wave with cleansing breath, follow with 6-9 chest inhalation-exhalations, conclude with cleansing breath

2

Accelerated Phase   45-60 Second Contractions

2-4 minute intervals between contractions

BREATHING

CONTRACTION

Take cleansing breath; accelerate breathing as wave rises, decelerate as it subsides; finish with a cleansing breath

3

Transitional Phase   60-90 Second Contractions

30-90 second intervals between contractions

BREATHING

CONTRACTION

Take cleansing breath; continue pattern of 4-6 breaths, then a short blowing out; take a final cleansing breath from 5 to 20 minutes. This first phase of labor, where the contractions are mild, lasts quite a long time. A study of the labor of many women has shown that the average time may be about 8 to 9 hours. For most of this period you will probably be at home, and you won't even need any breathing control for a great part of this phase.

If you are one of those very rare women who do have extremely easy and fast labors, you may not need every step of our training. But I would much rather have you prepare yourself for the average: a normal, lengthy labor. Should labor be faster than you anticipated, you will find that you are prepared to cope. For second or third babies, the average time limits for the three phases of the first stage of labor will be about half those of the first. Your actual contractions will feel the same, but the whole labor will be telescoped.

During the second, or *accelerated phase,* the waves of uterine contractions are higher, as you can see from the diagram, and the intervals between the contractions have shortened considerably. The length of one wave may be from 45 to 60 seconds by now, and the periods of rest are shorter, usually from 2 to 4 minutes.

The same study of the labor of many women has shown that the average length of time for the accelerated phase—the dilation of the cervix from about 3 to 8 centimeters or 1½ to 4 fingers—is about 3 to 4 hours.

The *transition* is the third phase of the first stage of labor. The contractions, represented as waves in our diagram, have become long, strong and erratic. They may have several peaks. They build up to maximum strength very quickly. They may last up to 1½ minutes, and the intervals between contractions are now shorter than the contractions themselves. The interval of rest may only be from 30 seconds to about 90 seconds. In fact, you may have just congratulated yourself that you managed to get through one of these contractions when you feel the next one already beginning. This, as you can imagine, is the hardest part of your labor. The only saving grace is that this phase is the shortest of the three subdivisions of the first stage of labor, and will usually last only from half an hour to an hour. I don't want to minimize the severity of the transitional contractions. You should be prepared for them and you should realize that this is like the final sprint of the uterine muscles. This period will demand more concentrated effort than any part previously experienced. But I will give you tools to work with and teach you how best to cope with this difficult part of your labor. One of my students reported to me one day on her labor. She said, "You talked of waves in labor, but it was a hurricane that hit me in transition."

The reason that I have given you approximate time limits for these phases of labor is to let you have some idea of what to expect. I cannot emphasize enough, however, that these are averages. There are many variations, all within the norm, and I want you to realize that it is very unlikely that your labor will be like any textbook description. Do not let this disturb you. In fact, it is one of the great advantages of the Lamaze technique that it provides the techniques to use as your individual labor demands. No two labors are the same. Even your own subsequent labors will differ and change in character from delivery to delivery.

THE FIRST TECHNIQUE OF BREATHING FOR THE FIRST STAGE OF LABOR

I will now give you three different breathing techniques to use during your first stage of labor. As you pass from preliminary labor, through accelerated labor, to the transition, you will adjust your breathing to the changes of the uterine contractions. I always think of this as if I were driving a car, shifting from first to second to third gear. It would never occur to you to

*To begin breathing practice, focus on fixed
object, breathe in through nose, out
through mouth; massage abdomen*

stay in first gear when you want to go faster. In the
same way, you will have to "shift gear" as your labor
progresses, in order to stay in control of your uterine
contractions.

And now to the first breathing technique you will
use in early labor. Be sure not to use this technique as
long as you can walk, talk or laugh through a contraction. You may get so excited at the onset of your
labor that you will want to breathe with it even if
there is no actual need. Please don't, because you will
soon become very bored by the whole process. Remember that the first phase can take hours and hours. You'd
be better off going for a walk with your husband, see-
ing a movie or tending to your usual house activities.
We often get so excited at the onset of labor that we

want to rush off to the hospital, hoping the baby will come quicker once we are there. Time, on the contrary, will seem endless if you arrive at the hospital too early. There is little in the labor room to divert your attention, and you may find this very demoralizing. At home, you will be more relaxed and fortified with the confidence your training has given you to handle the long latent part of labor. Of course, your own physician will give you exact instructions as to when he wants to be called. But my general advice is, don't rush.

Our aim during labor is to create a strong center of concentration through disciplined activity. The breathing technique we use has to be deliberate and different from our normal automatic breathing. I want you to breathe with your chest. Try it first by placing your hands flat under your breasts and letting your middle fingers meet. When you breathe with your chest, you will notice that your middle fingers will part slightly when you inhale and come together again when you exhale. Keep your abdomen relaxed while you breathe in this fashion. To make this chest breathing even more deliberate, I want you to inhale through your nose and exhale through your mouth. It's almost like whistling the air out. Take from 6 to 9 breaths in a minute, and count your breaths as you practice.

Begin every contraction by taking a deep cleansing breath. This will give you a good exchange of oxygen and carbon dioxide at the onset of a contraction, and at the same time relax you. Relaxation is a most important factor, as our usual reaction to a uterine contraction is what is called a "flight reaction." We tense our whole body. By taking a cleansing breath at the beginning of each contraction, you begin the contraction in a relaxed condition.

Now inhale through your nose, exhale through your lips, making a little noise with your breathing in order to keep a good rhythm. Count your breaths, and end each contraction with another cleansing breath. The relaxing breath at the end of each contraction is also of great importance. It means that you really come to a full stop, at the end of each contraction, emotionally and physically.

WHAT TO DO
WITH YOUR HANDS

It's very difficult to know what to do with one's hands in labor. You certainly should not grip the sides of your bed or dig your fingernails into your husband's arm. In order to avoid such tension, do what comes naturally and soothe the pain by massaging your abdomen gently in time to your breathing. This is the best way to do it: Cupping your hands lightly, place them under your abdomen. Then massage gently with your fingertips, leading your arms out and up while you inhale, completing the circle down again as you exhale. This massage, or "effleurage" as it is called professionally, not only provides another point of concentration, but also feels good. A light massage will help to relieve the tension in your abdomen during a contraction. It actually has the same effect as rubbing a place on your body that hurts. You can also try to massage your abdomen with one hand, using your whole hand gently. Or you may like to let your partner gently massage your belly. He can sit at your side and, using the palm of his hand, massage your abdomen slowly.

If you have to use a fetal monitor, which requires two belts around your belly, one for monitoring the fetal heart, the other for monitoring the uterine contraction, it will be difficult to use your hands in a circular movement over your abdomen. However, you will find that a gentle massage just over the lowest part of your abdomen will feel very soothing.

HYPERVENTILATION

Occasionally you may feel a little dizzy when you practice this deliberate breathing technique. We call this hyperventilation, or what happens when the balance between the oxygen intake and the carbon dioxide output is disturbed. During a prolonged practice session you may even feel a tingling or stiffening in your hands and feet or around your lips. It is unlikely, however, that this will happen in labor, as your uterus will need a great deal of oxygen while it is contracting. But just in case, here are two easy ways to overcome this: Cup your hands, hold them over your nose and mouth and breathe in your own carbon dioxide; or hold your breath for a few seconds when the contraction is over. This will soon accumulate enough carbon dioxide, and your dizziness will quickly disappear. Hyperventilation is most likely to occur in labor during the *accelerated* and *transition* stages.

I suggest that if you become hyperventilated at the hospital and do not want to hold your breath, use a little paper sandwich bag to breathe into. This will be more effective than using your hands. And since you are going to bring this little paper bag along, there are a few things you can add to it which may be useful during labor. One of these is a small can of talcum powder. In actual labor you will be massaging your skin during each contraction. Your fingers may get hot and sticky. You may irritate your abdomen after a long period of massaging. Use the talcum powder on your abdomen or your hands to avoid such excessive friction. Let your partner sprinkle it on whenever you need it. (Later we'll discover many other things to carry along in our Lamaze bag.)

Keep your eyes open during a contraction and while practicing the breathing technique. Be sure, however, to focus on one point in the room. This will help you to concentrate. You will find that nothing happening outside your line of vision will concern you. It is vitally important to maintain this discipline in your practice session since during real labor you will need every ounce of concentration. An even better way would be to have eye contact with your partner. He could then work easily with you and correct your breathing when necessary. You may find that in practicing the eye contact with him, you'll probably break up laughing. But to tell the truth, I've never seen anybody laugh or giggle through labor, though I must admit that would be a great way to have a baby!

POSITION OF BODY DURING EARLY LABOR

You do not have to lie down when you are in labor. We always assume that the moment we go into the hospital we have to lie down in a bed and behave like a very sick person. I want you to remember that having a baby is a healthy event, and that the only reason we go to a hospital is because it is safer, not because we are suffering from a disease. I realize it isn't easy to overcome the notion that hospitals are places where one must suffer.

It is interesting to remember that forty to fifty years ago, when most women delivered their babies at home, nobody would have thought to call a laboring woman "a patient." She was just "a woman in labor" or "a woman giving birth to her child." It was only when women were encouraged to have their babies in hospitals that the laboring woman was called a "patient," a term that obviously makes us think of illness and suffering.

In fact, with the introduction of the episiotomy (a small surgical incision in the area between vagina and anus to allow the baby to emerge more easily and without tearing), having a baby actually became a surgical procedure.

Many hospitals insist that when you enter—having walked comfortably from your car or taxi into the hospital lobby—you must immediately get into a wheelchair. This may make you feel apprehensive straight away. You are likely to remember all the old tales of suffering in childbirth. But try to realize that once you enter the hospital, the hospital is responsible for your well-being. Even if you have to sit in a wheelchair, take the ride to the labor room in good humor and don't let it depress you.

In the labor room you will be asked to undress and put on a hospital gown, which is usually not attractive at all. I know you would much rather wear your own pretty gown. But remember that this hospital gown is functional, serves a good purpose and is far more practical to wear during labor than your own.

When the attending nurse asks you to get into bed, you will see a bed similar to yours at home (with just one pillow) although it may be a bit higher, for the convenience of the doctors and nurses. Don't forget that all hospital beds can be rolled up. Ask your nurse to roll it to any angle that is comfortable. Most of us can breathe much better with our heads raised, or even sitting up, and there is no reason you should not experiment in order to find your own comfortable position. You may want to lie on your side, sit up tailor fashion, legs crossed, or recline at any angle that suits you. You will only have to lie flat when you are being examined or when your physician suggests a certain position that he prefers you to be in.

MAN'S ROLE
DURING PRACTICE

When you practice the first breathing technique at home, let your partner give you precise commands. He should have a stop watch with a sweep second hand to time you. Practice the breathing for approximately one minute—occasionally varying the time from 40 to 60 seconds to imitate the length of a real contraction. It is extremely important that your partner be as precise in his commands as you will have to be in your performance. Therefore he has to give the command: *contraction begins* and then *contraction ends,* and not just say "start" and "stop." This is important because you are training yourself to react to a uterine contraction with a respiratory response instead of a flight response. We are using therefore what is called "secondary conditioning," which means the correct command has to trigger your reaction.

It will also be helpful if your partner calls off the seconds while you practice your breathing. He should say: "Contraction begins," and then call out, "15 seconds . . . 30 seconds . . . 45 seconds . . . contraction ends." You will find this a very helpful device. It will make the contraction seem shorter. When your partner calls out 30 seconds, you will know that you are at the halfway point and when he says 45 seconds, it will mean "going, going, going, gone." Many couples find this not only useful during practice sessions, but also in actual labor. Your partner's signal at that time will be your cleansing breath. From this he will know that you have started another contraction. He will then look at his watch and call out the seconds for you. Try it and see how you like it.

Now let's practice the first breathing technique.

Take up any position that is comfortable for you. Contraction begins. Take a deep, relaxing, cleansing breath. Breathe in through your nose, and slowly exhale through your lips. Count your breaths, focus your eyes on a point in the room, or even better have eye contact with your partner, and massage your abdomen lightly with your fingertips, out and up as you inhale, down as you exhale. Or let your partner gently massage your abdomen. Finish with a deep cleansing breath.

It is both important and helpful for the partner to supervise his partner while she practices her breathing

Be sure to keep the rest of your body as relaxed as possible while practicing.

When you practice by yourself, give yourself commands—contraction begins, contraction ends—and follow the time on a clock with a second hand. Also visualize the pictures and diagrams that show contractions, so that it will be clear in your mind how your body is working at the time. It always helps to imagine the wave of a contraction and how you will ride the wave with your breathing technique. And be sure to practice your breathing with any Braxton-Hicks contraction that you may feel.

LESSON 4

What to do for back labor; breathing
techniques two and three, for the
accelerated and transitional phases; how
the partner can simulate a contraction

We will begin by reviewing what you have learned in the previous lessons. I expect you to carry on with the neuromuscular control exercises, so you can improve your body control and you and your partner can develop good teamwork. I am sure you will have noticed by now that the body-building exercises are no longer so tiring. In fact, you probably feel better for performing them and strengthening these muscles that have to carry most of the strain during pregnancy.

And now again to our first breathing technique. Do you think that by now you can describe our first technique to a friend who has never heard of it? You would have to begin by telling her that we divide the first stage of labor into three parts. They are: 1) The preliminary or latent part of labor, in which the cervix effaces and starts to dilate. 2) The accelerated part of labor, in which the cervix dilates approximately from 3 to 8 centimeters, or 1½ to 4 fingers. And, finally 3) The transition, in which the cervix dilates from approximately 8 to 10 centimeters, or 4 to 5 fingers. The waves of uterine contractions change in character as labor progresses, and you will remember that you must synchronize your breathing techniques with the intensity of the sensations that you will feel.

Then you must tell your friend what the actual breathing technique is like. We begin the contraction by taking a deep, relaxing, cleansing breath. This is followed by deliberate chest breathing, inhaling through the nose, exhaling through the mouth. We finish, when the contraction subsides, with another deep, relaxing, cleansing breath. We take any position that is comfortable, concentrating on one point in the room or having eye contact. At the same time we effleurage, or massage, our abdomen, moving our fingertips lightly in a circular motion to the rhythm of our breathing, or we encourage our partner to massage our abdomen gently.

Now try the breathing once again while I give the commands: Contraction begins. Take a deep, cleansing breath. Now breathe comfortably and deliberately with your chest, inhale through your nose, exhale through your mouth, 15 seconds, 30 seconds, 45 seconds . . . the contraction is over. End with a deep cleansing breath. Did you have between 6 and 9 breaths during this simulated contraction?

WHERE DO YOU FEEL A CONTRACTION?

I wonder if you have ever thought about where in your abdomen you will actually feel a contraction? Will you feel it all over, just low down, or perhaps in the back? Actually, the majority of women feel their labor low down, just above the pubic bone, but deep inside and spreading towards the groin. Some may feel a contraction beginning in the lower back and radiating to the lower abdomen, even drawing into the thighs. If you feel your labor in your legs, massage your legs! Don't get stuck rubbing your belly when most of the pain is in your thighs. Remember, I give you the tools to work with, but it will be up to you, according to your labor, to decide how and when you use the tools. All this demands a great flexibility on your part, but it also makes sense that you react to your body and its own rhythm instead of to what I have said or what you may have read in a textbook.

I remember being woken one morning by a telephone call. An excited voice was saying, "Mrs. Bing, Mrs. Bing, we are in the hospital and it's all in Charlotte's legs! What can we do?" I managed to open my eyes and say sleepily, "Massage her thighs." "Oh," said the voice on the other end of the line. Then I heard a click and I could see in my mind how he was racing upstairs to massage Charlotte's thighs. About twenty-five per cent of women experience what is called "back labor." I want you all to be aware of the fact that back labor exists. I am sure this may come as a surprise for many of you. After all, why should one feel anything in the back, when one imagines that the uterus is right here in front in the abdomen? Obviously the baby is there in front too, and the most natural thing would be to expect labor where one imagines the baby and uterus to be.

There is no one cause for back labor. However, it most often occurs when the baby lies in a posterior position: the baby is facing the mother's abdomen with the back of his head pressed against her spine. It is important, therefore, for you to be prepared for a possible experience of back labor.

WAYS TO ALLEVIATE BACK LABOR

Now what can we do about back labor? Your breathing technique should remain the same, whether you feel contractions in your abdomen or in your back. However, it is possible to alleviate the discomfort of back labor in a number of ways:

1. counter pressure
2. change of position
3. change of temperature

1. Instead of massaging your abdomen, you can massage or put pressure on your back. Back labor is usually felt in two distinct points low on your back, near the sacrum.

Massaging your back is fine, but does not really help you to relax. Your partner's help at this point will be invaluable. He can massage your back, or put counter pressure against the points that hurt during a contraction. He can put a good deal of pressure on your back and need not worry about hurting you at all. The uterus is far away from the area he will be pressing against. In fact, the more pressure he exerts against the painful areas, the better you will feel.

When your partner has been pressing his fists into your back for two hours or more, not only will his back be sore, but his knuckles will be rubbed through. We therefore suggest that you bring two tennis balls or a can of tennis balls to lean against and give your husband a rest. Actually, anything hard will do the trick. The tennis balls will give the counter pressure in your back and relieve some of the back pain.

Tell your partner he does not have to worry about finding the right spot to press against. You are sure to tell him in no uncertain terms to move his hand or fist to the left, to the right, to the middle, or up or down.

2. Change your position. What would you think the aim in changing position to be? The simple answer is: Get the baby off your back! As long as you are half sitting or perhaps even lying on your back, you have the weight of the baby on your spine, which definitely aggravates back labor. You will probably find it far more comfortable to lie on your side, allowing the weight of the baby to be carried by the bed. Bend both knees, placing the upper knee in front of the lower one, and support the upper knee with a pillow. It is best to lie on the side of the "occiput," which means the side where the back of the baby's head is. If you cannot tell where the baby's head is, do not hesitate to ask the attending nurse or your physician. You may also feel perfectly comfortable sitting up at an angle of 90 degrees. Have your husband roll up your bed, but do not lean against the back of the bed. Round your back and put a pillow for support against the lower part of your spine.

Another position which some women find helpful is what we call the "knee-chest" position. You kneel and rest your body on your lower arms and hands. In this position the weight of the baby is entirely off your spine, and may provide excellent relief from all back pressure. Many women also use this position when suffering from severe menstrual cramps. A very good variation here would be to kneel on the bed and at the same time to lean against the rolled-up bed. In this position, the weight of the baby would be off your spine, gravity would help to move the baby down, and the pressure of the baby's head against the cervix might help the dilation. Try out these positions and practice the breathing exercises with them—this way you will be prepared for any changes that may occur during your labor.

You could also sit on the edge of the bed, feet resting on a chair. Use the bed table with a pillow to rest your arms and shoulders. This will be less tiring than the kneeling position.

One way to alleviate discomfort in back labor is to lie on your side with partner exerting pressure on lower back

When taking the side position for back
labor, be sure to bend both knees
and elevate the upper leg to avoid stress

Kneeling on bed and leaning against raised head
of bed is an excellent position for back labor

3. While you are still at home, during the early stages of labor, you may find a heating pad or hot-water bottle very beneficial for back labor. I am afraid we are usually not allowed to use heating pads in the hospital.

In the hospital you could use a coolpack or Scotch ice or any of the picnic coolers that you can freeze beforehand in the freezing compartment of your refrigerator. Freezing, i.e., anesthetizing the area that hurts with a cold compress, may relieve back pain.

All these methods alleviate the discomfort of back labor. You will have to experiment once you are in labor and discover which method is best for you.

SECOND BREATHING TECHNIQUE

We will now discuss the second part of the first stage of labor, a period during which the cervix dilates from 3 to 8 centimeters. Contractions are now becoming stronger, they last from 45 to 60 seconds, the intervals are now less than 5 minutes, most likely between 2 and 3 minutes. First-phase breathing is usually no longer effective once contractions have reached this accelerated pace. You will now need a second tool to control the strong waves. Let's say we have to shift into second gear.

Our aim must be to speed up the breathing, making it much more shallow, as if beginning a fast sprint. If one starts running, one's breathing speeds up. In this accelerated phase, the uterus works harder, and you must react to this with more rapid breathing. This allows the hard-working uterine muscle to function more efficiently and also to bring more oxygen to the uterus and to your baby.

I want to give you a few pointers before you try out this faster, shallow breathing.

Start, as always, with a deep, relaxing, cleansing breath. You can do this breathing either through your mouth or through your nose. The advantage of practicing it through your nose is that your throat and mouth will not get so dry. It is up to you however. If you try breathing through your mouth, keep both passages open so that you will always feel a little air coming through your nose as well. This helps a great deal in relaxing the facial muscles. Breathe lightly and evenly, accentuating your exhalation slightly. You will find that the inhalation is a reflex; but you will have to concentrate on making the exhalation short and staccato, so that your breaths stay shallow and even. Breathe quietly; in fact, don't make any noise at all.

Remember to keep your neck muscles relaxed. Open your mouth very slightly, almost as if you were smiling. This will help you do this breathing almost in your throat.

Try this breathing technique very slowly at first. It may help you to beat a rhythm with your fingers. It has also helped some women to breathe in certain rhythms, stressing every first breath in four—for example, a little song in 4/4 rhythm. I've found that "Yankee Doodle" gives a wonderful beat to breathe too. Be sure to make the "Yankee Doodle" very "moderato." If you find yourself going "allegro vivace," you can be sure your breathing is much too fast. I'd rather have you err on the slow side than breathe too fast.

Don't be too ambitious when you first try this breathing technique. It is easy to become discouraged. Remember that it is quite difficult, and must be practiced over a long period of time. I would advise you to try it several times a day. Begin by doing it for 15 seconds only, then increase it to 30 seconds. Eventually you should be able to breathe easily and evenly for about 45 seconds to a minute without undue fatigue. If you lose the rhythm, overexpand your chest by breathing in more air than you breathe out, or if you get tired, blow out all the air in your lungs and resume the breathing immediately. Always begin and end your practice with a cleansing breath.

SECOND BREATHING
TECHNIQUE IN LABOR

Now I am going to show you how to apply this new breathing technique in labor.

Look again at the diagram showing the second part of the first stage of labor, the accelerated phase. The waves representing intensity of contraction are fairly high. You will see from the drawing that each wave increases in intensity as it rises and decreases in intensity as it subsides.

Your task at this point is to follow the wave of the contraction. There is no sense in exhausting yourself by breathing rapidly from beginning to end of the wave. Remember that one of our main objectives is to channel our energies and be as economical as possible with our muscle power.

You must therefore start the contraction with a cleansing breath and then start to breathe slowly, increasing your rate of breathing as the contraction increases in intensity. Breathe in a 4/4 rhythm at the peak of the contraction, but immediately slow down your breathing as the contraction tapers off. Conclude with another cleansing breath. In this way you will stay with the wave, accelerating when the contraction builds up and decelerating as it subsides. It is as if you are running a race with the contraction, but a race in which you must only keep parallel.

I will now give you the commands for this second breathing technique. Contraction begins: focus your eyes on one point or have eye contact with your partner. Take a cleansing breath and relax your whole body. Start to breathe slowly but take shallow breaths. Now the contraction is getting stronger, stronger, stronger. It is at its peak. It is still at its peak. It is still there. It is still there, and now it begins to subside, slower and slower and slower and slower. Contraction is over. Take a deep cleansing breath.

After you have practiced accelerating and decelerating your breathing for a few days, I want you to add the effleurage, or massage of your abdomen. This is difficult and needs a great deal of coordination, as the massage has to be performed slowly, regularly and lightly, as your breathing builds up and slows down.

When practicing this breathing by yourself, I want you to give exact commands in your own mind. Watch a clock with a second hand, and say to yourself "Contraction begins!" Then slowly increase your rate of breathing so that you get to the peak within 10 to 15 seconds, stay at the peak for about 20 to 30 seconds, slow down for 15 to 20 seconds. Conclude by saying "Contraction ends!"

YOUR PARTNER SIMULATES A CONTRACTION

If your partner practices with you, let him put his hand just above your knee, and as he gives you the command "Contraction begins!" let him put pressure on your thigh. He should increase the pressure slowly, coming to the peak of his pressure in about 10 to 15 seconds, keeping it up for about 20 to 30 seconds, then reducing the pressure slowly for about another 15 to 20 seconds.

In this way we are simulating, in a sense, a uterine contraction. You will be reacting to an actual physical discomfort which increases in intensity, comes to a peak and decreases again. Try it. After you have tried this, ask your partner to press your leg once while you're not panting, just as hard as he did it before. I am sure you will discover that the pressure is quite a painful sensation without your breathing technique.

*Bill simulates a contraction by putting
hard pressure above Gail's knee.
Correct breathing eliminates her discomfort*

Practice in different positions in order to be prepared for labor and be sure to be absolutely relaxed at all times. Also remind your partner to watch you closely, and correct any mistakes he sees.

THE TRANSITION

You will remember that during the transition period the cervix dilates from about 7 or 8 centimeters to 10 centimeters, or 3½ or 4 to 5 fingers. The contractions are now more severe than at any previous time. Before I tell you about the breathing for the transition period, I want to mention some symptoms that may occur during this phase of your labor.

1. Frequently there is a bloody, mucous discharge at

this time. Nurses often call this a "good bloody show." This is caused by pressure from the baby's head against the cervix, which is extremely sensitive and has many delicate, superficial blood vessels. These little blood vessels may break. You will suddenly notice that you are getting rather wet. It is important for you and your partner to know that a "bloody show" at this point is normal. In fact it is a sign that the baby's head is descending and that you are getting closer to full dilation, and the second stage of labor.

2. Most women will feel an increasing amount of pressure in the rectum at this point. You may also have back labor, even if up to now you have felt labor only in your lower abdomen. You may find that sitting upright and leaning slightly forward will alleviate a great deal of back pressure, or perhaps even lying on your side. Also, instead of massaging your abdomen, put your hands over your coccyx (the lowest vertebra of your spine) and press hard. Better still, let your partner press upward against your coccyx.

3. It is possible that you will already feel a slight desire to push at this point. However, it is most important that you do not push until your physician has examined you and given explicit permission to do so. The desire to push is a reflex set off by pressure of the baby's head against the vaginal walls, the rectum and the pelvic floor. Occasionally this reflex occurs before you are fully dilated. It is imperative, therefore, that you act against this reflex and don't push until dilation is complete. If you try to push the baby through an opening that is too small, you will have unnecessary pain, you will waste a great deal of valuable effort and you will risk a swelling of your cervix.

There is a very easy way to counteract the urge to push. It can be done by forcibly exhaling, or blowing out air until the urge has passed. You know, of course, that when you try to expel a stool, you hold your breath. Even if you are lifting a heavy weight, you hold your breath to do so.

Try the following exercise: Hold your breath and strain. Now blow out continuously, always breathing in and out, and try to strain at the same time. Notice that this is almost impossible. You will understand now why I ask you to blow out forcibly and continually during labor whenever you get an early urge to push and have been told not to.

4. Some women feel nauseated during transition and may even vomit. Please realize that if this should happen to you, these unpleasant symptoms are within the normal course of events. Don't be frightened if they occur.

5. Occasionally a woman will start to shake or tremble. You may find that it becomes more and more difficult to relax. You may feel hot and cold, and your control of the uterine waves may become more and more difficult.

I would like to tell you about one of my students whom I had warned about these possible unpleasant symptoms during the transition period. Apparently she had not really believed that anything like that could happen to her. But there she was in transition, her legs shaking like a leaf. She didn't become frightened, but she thought it was so funny that she started to laugh. She kept on pointing at her trembling legs and laughing. The nurse in attendance thought my student had lost her mind. She had certainly never before seen anybody laugh during the transition.

6. Finally, there is one more symptom I want to mention. Almost every woman gets terribly irritable during this phase of labor. Up to now you have been grateful for your partner's help: his rubbing your back, wetting your lips with a sponge, encouraging you. Now suddenly you may find yourself snapping at him: "Don't touch me. Don't talk to me, leave me alone!" Partners must be aware of this possibility and remember that this bad temper is only temporary. It will disappear as soon as you are fully dilated and have been given permission to push.

BREATHING
DURING TRANSITION

In order to stay in control during these extremely strong contractions, we need a new breathing technique which is even more precise and demands even more concentrated effort on our part. A stronger, more forceful rhythm has to be established. As an obstetrician once observed, "You have to become Rockettes in labor," which means that you have to work with the kind of precision the Rockettes use in Radio City Music Hall. We can do this best by using four or six or eight short breaths, followed by a quick exhalation (through pursed lips), continuing this pattern until the end of the contraction, which may now last as long as 1½ minutes.

The short exhalation after 4, 6, or 8 breaths should be just like a short accent. Be sure to make it quite short—don't rest on it by breathing too slowly. Do not forget to use the cleansing breath here at the beginning and end of the contraction. These strong transition contractions are likely to reach the peak of their intensity within 1 or 2 seconds of the beginning, so you will have no time to accelerate slowly. Use the very rapid breathing immediately after the cleansing breath, and only slow down when the contraction begins to taper off. Do not massage your abdomen any more during this period, but do have a specific place for your hands. Support your abdomen with them, for example, putting slight pressure on your groin. Or you may prefer pressing your hands against your coccyx.

Should you feel a desire to push during such a contraction, blow out continuously, remembering to breathe in after each forcible exhalation. Then return to the breathe-and-blow pattern, once the urge to push has subsided, for as long as the contraction continues.

*Gail practices third breathing technique
by establishing a strict pattern;
6 quick breaths followed by a short blow*

I suggest that you use the transition breathing once your contractions begin to come as rapidly as 1½ minutes apart, regardless of whether you experience any of the other symptoms mentioned above.

Remember that you must react to your specific uterine contractions and not to a preconceived idea of what your labor should be like. Let me repeat again: every labor is different from every other. You may experience innumerable variations of my description of labor. But the great advantage of the Lamaze technique is that it provides you with enough techniques to stay in control of your labor, however it may vary from your expectations.

I will now give the command: Contraction begins; cleansing breath; rapid breathing—1, 2, 3, 4, 5, 6, exhale (*do not blow out too much air or you may hyperventilate*) 1, 2, 3, 4, 5, 6, blow out, 1, 2, 3, etc.

Contraction over, cleansing breath . . . and rest. Make the most of the rest between contractions. Save energy!

Here is some advice to the coach. It happens frequently that your partner will suddenly say, "I've had enough, I'm giving up, I can't make it" or something to that effect. Go and get the nurse or doctor and ask him or her to examine your wife. The chances are she is either fully dilated or 5–10 minutes away from it.

The untrained woman will feel like giving up at 5- or 6-centimeter dilation. The trained woman will want to quit when she is almost ready to push her baby out.

This rapid breathing will make you thirsty, particularly if you breathe through your mouth. Many hospitals will not allow you to drink anything during labor except an occasional sip of water. If you are lucky you may be offered some crushed ice. I advise you, therefore, to bring some lollipops or a peppermint stick to the hospital, so that you can lubricate your mouth a little between contractions.

You can bring a "Lamaze bag," which can, of course, be any old shopping bag, and which will hold your can of talcum powder, the lollipops or peppermint sticks, a small paper bag to breathe in in case you hyperventilate, and some other items which you will find on the complete list on page 112.

LESSON 5

The second stage of labor; what happens
during actual delivery and how to
prepare for it; partner's role during
delivery; how to stop pushing on command

We have now covered the entire first stage of labor, and you have learned the techniques that will be used during this long period. Before discussing the second stage, or expulsion, it is imperative to review all our exercises, relaxation techniques and breathing methods.

Do you remember what to do if you have back labor? You will recall that the breathing techniques remain the same whether your labor is felt in your abdomen or your back, and that there are changes of position that will help. You should roll your bed up to an angle of 90 degrees. Do not lean back, but bend slightly forward, and put a pillow against your lower back. This will help to take the weight of the baby off your spine. You may prefer instead to try lying on your side, your upper knee resting on a pillow over the lower knee. Another technique is the knee-chest position, in which you lean forward on all fours with your lower arms resting on a pillow, or one in which you kneel on the bed, leaning your arms and trunk against the raised bed. Or sit on the edge of your bed, feet resting on a chair, and support your arms and shoulders on a table.

We have also seen how you can ease back labor by exerting pressure on your lower back with your fingers or fists. Or your partner may massage you, pressing his hands as hard as he can against the lower part of your spine. Or you can use the tennis balls you brought along in your "Lamaze bag."

If you have back labor during transition, the kneeling position, leaning against the raised bed, may be most comfortable. But in the final analysis, it will always have to be you who decides which position, counter pressure or cold application is the most comforting at the time. If there is a great deal of rectal pressure, ask your partner or the nurse to push against your coccyx. Remember that about 25 per cent of women experience back labor, so it's important to be well prepared for this possibility.

Now practice the three breathing techniques for the first stage of labor. I'm sure you will notice how much you've improved in the week or two that you have been practicing. The rapid shallow breathing should be easier to perform, your rhythm should be better—and now you probably don't get too exhausted. During the stress of actual labor your breathing will come quite easily—automatically, in fact. All your practice and training will help you to coordinate your activities, channel your energy and use your body with a minimum amount of effort.

THE SECOND
STAGE OF LABOR

Expulsion is really the most wonderful stage of labor. Until now you've worked hard, concentrating on riding each wave of your contractions. You've had to relax under great stress and still perform your breathing techniques. And all this has probably gone on for a good number of hours.

During the second stage you will *still* have to work tremendously hard. But now you can help your uterus in the expulsion of your baby. It is the most satisfying and exhilarating work you will ever have to do. This stage is much shorter than the long, tedious dilation of the cervix, and you know that your baby will soon be born. You will feel during this period as if you have a second wind. Although the expulsion will be just about the hardest physical work you'll ever do in your life, it will feel absolutely wonderful.

Before I explain the technique of pushing, I want you to look again at the illustration showing the expulsion of the baby, so that you will understand the workings of your uterus, how the baby is being rotated and how you can help with the expulsion—consciously, in order to expel your baby smoothly. You will be able to do this, because you have been practicing the pelvic floor exercises for many weeks.

At this point you will see again how important the Kegel exercises have been to prepare your body for the expulsion of your baby.

Once the baby is descending, there will be great pressure on your rectum. It is now imperative for you to be able to relax the pelvic floor.

WHAT HAPPENS
DURING DELIVERY

Look once again at the illustrations and visualize how the baby is expelled from the uterus. Think also of how you can help with your own pushing to bring the baby out as smoothly and quickly as possible. You can see that as the baby enters the vagina, or birth canal, it rotates 90 degrees, and now faces the mother's spine. The baby's head bends down when it reaches the pelvic floor, so that the crown of its head shows first at the exit of the vagina, or vulva. You can see now why the doctor will talk of "the baby's head crowning."

If it is your first baby you will start pushing in the labor room and be moved to the delivery room only when about a dime-sized area of the head is showing. At this point your husband will probably be able to tell you what color hair the baby has. To push the baby down this far may take anywhere from 10 to 30 minutes. Then—in the delivery room—the baby's head will bend back as it stretches the outlet of the vagina, and you will push it out. This should take another 15 to 20 minutes, assuming that there are no complications. If this is your second or third or even fourth pregnancy, you will be moved into the delivery room as soon as you are fully dilated and have been given permission to push.

Now you'll need the action of the diaphragm to give additional force to the uterus in its expulsive action. You can reinforce the uterus by using your upper abdominal muscles, and by forcing down the diaphragm to help from above. Pushing the baby out is like piston action: hard pressure from above pushing down and out. Your aim now is to reduce the intra-abdominal space and to increase the intra-abdominal pressure.

This action could be best accomplished if you were allowed to assume a squatting position to expel the baby. It is interesting that about two-thirds of the women on our earth *still* give birth in the squatting position. I think we would never have to teach a woman to bear down if we could let her push the baby out while squatting. Unfortunately, modern society and modern obstetric technique demand of us that we push lying down, really against gravity and against normal instinct. Of course, it is easier for the attending physician to deal with any difficulties that may occur if the woman is lying on her back with legs raised. However, position and even designs for delivery tables are now slowly changing; that is to say, changing in such a way that the comfort of the delivering mother is considered. A new concept, the Lamaze labor-delivery-bed, has been accepted by now in a number of hospitals all over the country.

Such a labor-delivery-bed would not only allow the mother to labor and deliver in one bed and one place, which would afford her a far more effective and smoother effort, especially during the delivery of her baby, but it would also allow her to have her back raised and supported and to have her legs supported at a level lower than is possible on a regular delivery table. Her position would be something like this.

You can see how much more logical and physiologically sound such a position would be, and also how much more comfortable the mother would be. Surely, no other mammal on this earth is asked to give birth lying flat on its back with its legs up in the air!

But as the majority of women will still have to start their pushing in the labor room and then be moved onto a regular delivery table once a little of the head is showing, I will explain to you now how to practice the pushing in the labor bed.

Practice Pushing at Home for the Labor Room

Lean against your partner's legs, sitting on your tail bone at an angle of about 75 degrees from the horizontal. Rest your feet on the floor, feet and knees comfortably separated. Hold on to your knees or under your knees. Keep your elbows well out and push your head forward. Your back should be rounded as it is resting against your partner's legs.

It is important that you push correctly and in a disciplined fashion so that you can expel the baby in as short a period as possible. You will have to push only with contractions and only when you have been given the okay for pushing by some one in authority, i.e., a nurse, a resident or your doctor.

The contractions will slow down somewhat when you start to push. They will probably not be as violent as your transition contraction. Don't rush into pushing. You will be more effective if you do it slowly and deliberately. Now, let us assume a contraction begins. As usual, we start by taking a deep cleansing breath. However, to get the most out of a contraction, let it build up strength first before you help the uterus in its expulsion effort. Therefore, take a second cleansing breath. Then inhale a third time deeply, let out a little of your breath, hold the remaining air, relax your lower jaw and push steadily, directing all your force through your vagina. Remember, elbows out, head forward, pelvic floor muscles relaxed. Sustain the pushing effort for 10–15 seconds, let the air out, lower your head, quickly take another breath, exhale a little, hold the rest and bear down, relax your lower jaw, hold and push for 10–15 seconds, breathe out and let your head relax. Quickly take a third breath, exhale a little, hold the rest, relax your lower jaw, and push smoothly for 10–15 seconds, thinking in the direction of your vagina. Finally breathe out, and take several cleansing breaths to make up for the oxygen you didn't bring to the baby while you were pushing.

In this way you are helping the uterus by giving it direction and added force from above, while at the same time removing resistance from below. This is extremely hard work!

You can practice the pushing exercise safely every day, holding your breath for 10–15 seconds only. During actual labor, however, you will have to sustain your pushing efforts for a longer period. Usually you'll need three breaths and three pushes for one contraction. And in actual labor you will reinforce your uterus with deliberate muscular efforts. Each time you push, the baby will descend a certain distance, and each time the contraction is over the baby will slip back a little. It's really like taking two steps forward and one back. Therefore, the more force you can exert against the uterus from above and the more you can relax your pelvic-floor muscles from below, the faster your baby will be born.

PARTNER'S ROLE DURING EXPULSION

Your partner can be of great assistance in practicing this technique. He can make sure you are in a correct position. He can support your back. He can practice with you and give the pushing commands: "Breathe in —breathe out, breathe in—breathe out, breathe in—let out a litle air—hold your remaining breath, hold on to your legs, open them wide, keep your elbows out, raise your head, relax your lower lip, and push, push, push . . . breathe out—take a second breath, let out a little, hold your breath, relax your lower jaw and push . . . push . . . breathe out, quickly once more: breathe in, let out a little—hold, relax your lower lip and push, push . . . breath out and relax."

I have found that even the best-trained woman may forget how to push. The doctor gives her the permission to push with the next contraction, and she will suddenly look up in utter panic and say: "I've forgotten how!" It is unlikely that both of you will forget the same things at the same time, and it will help you enormously if your partner can give you exact commands. You'll have to tell him when the contraction begins, and he will then give you the signals when to breathe and push. I am sure that once he has done this for two or three contractions, you'll be able to function perfectly well on your own.

Try not to be too much of a perfectionist in labor. It may take you a few contractions until you really feel that you are pushing well. Don't be discouraged. You will fall into the correct pattern of pushing very quickly, particularly if you and your partner have trained together and are allowed to work together during labor and delivery.

THE DELIVERY-ROOM TABLE

The pushing technique that you will use on the delivery table is the same that you used in the labor room. The delivery-room table is very much like the table in your doctor's office: hard, flat and narow. But instead of putting your heels into stirrups, as you do in your doctor's office, your legs will be supported under your knees and thighs. This is much more comfortable. Unfortunately, in most hospitals the delivery table cannot be raised so that you can push down from above. You should therefore ask your doctor if you may bring your pillows from the labor room into the delivery room to support your shoulders and head. A few hospitals may provide a backrest on the delivery table or a foam-rubber bolster.

You will have handles or grips to hold onto, or you may hold the vertical bars that attach the stirrups to the table. These handles or bars will enable you to pull yourself up when you have to push.

In order to allow for the most comfortable position to push, ask that the stirrups be lowered, so that you can raise your back to an angle of about 40–45 degrees. If the table cannot be raised, or if there is no backrest available, push the pillows you've brought from the labor room well under your back, not just under your head and shoulders.

It is of great advantage to practice pushing in the actual positions you're likely to use during real labor. In this way, you can train your body and muscles to function well in the proper positions from the very beginning.

When you are on the delivery table your legs and your abdomen will be draped with sterile material. Be sure never to touch the sterile drapes! Keep your hands firmly on the bars. It used to be common to strap a woman's wrists in order to make sure that she would not inadvertently touch the sterile drapes placed over her abdomen and legs. However, most physicians and nurses will not insist on restraining your hands. They know that a trained woman will not touch any drapes or sheets she has been asked not to touch. It will be difficult for you to watch the emergence of your child, because you are too low and the drape obstructs your view. But frequently there is a mirror above the delivery table, which can be easily adjusted so that you can watch your baby being born.

HOW TO STOP PUSHING ON COMMAND

At the moment your baby's head emerges and begins rotating to allow the shoulders to come out, your doctor may tell you to stop pushing. It is of the utmost importance that you are prepared to cooperate immediately. Lean back, relax your body and blow out repeatedly until the urge to push is over. In a short time your doctor will advise you to continue pushing for the shoulders, but this pause is likely to be a difficult moment for you. The urge to push will probably be extremely strong and you will be asked to counteract this strong involuntary feeling. It's quite possible to prepare for this moment if, in your expulsion exercises at home, you let your husband occasionally give you the command "stop pushing," and you learn to react instantaneously.

Gail and Bill practice the labor room pushing
with Gail's back at about a 75° angle

Barbara and Tom practice the delivery room pushing
with Barbara's back at about a 35° angle

LESSON 6

Recognizing real labor; what to bring
along; moment-to-moment at the hospital;
breathing with your labor; use of
medication; the great moment and after

I'm sure you have often wondered: How will I know when my labor begins? How will I be able to tell the difference between the kind of contractions I've been having for the last few weeks and the real ones? I've heard that perhaps I can sleep through part of my labor —is this true?

These are very legitimate questions. One good basic rule to follow is this: when you feel slight contractions and you are not sure whether this is real labor or not, the chances are it is *not*. Yes, you can sleep through early labor, but any contraction that doesn't wake you is obviously so mild that you don't have to concentrate on it. I have often found that the doctor and the laboring mother do not agree on when labor started. For the woman, it feels like labor when the contractions are obvious enough for her to be aware of them. They may be mild, but she is excited, she knows she should not eat any more, and she listens carefully to every little sign and symptom her body gives her. Finally she wants to know for certain and calls the doctor, who may tell her to come to the hospital to be examined. She arrives at the hospital and is examined, and the doctor tells her that she is not in labor yet.

This is very upsetting. She has been having contractions for hours by now, she has not eaten anything, she has been awake most of the night, and now the doctor tells her that this is not labor yet. What are those contractions, and when will they become effective so that the cervix begins to dilate? she asks herself. She is already tired, and the doctor tells her she has not even started labor yet. This can be a difficult time.

There are, however, certain definite indications that you should be aware of. Therefore I would like to discuss with you now the signs with which we associate the beginning of labor.

1. You may observe an increase in mucous discharge towards the end of your pregnancy. At one point this discharge will probably be tinged with a little blood. This will indicate the expulsion of the mucous plug which closes the cervix during your pregnancy. It is generally just a very slight stain, which you will notice only when you go to the bathroom. If no other symptoms—such as contractions or breaking of the membrane—occur simultaneously, don't get too excited at this point. It may be hours or even days before you will go into real labor. Therefore, losing the mucous plug is not necessarily a reliable indication of the beginning of labor.

2. The second indication of the beginning of labor is the onset of actual contractions. Contractions do not always start as the textbooks tell us: first about 20 minutes apart, gradually getting closer together and becoming more regular. It is just as normal for the contractions to begin only 5 minutes apart. Do not become alarmed if this occurs. It is a perfectly normal variation. It *is* important that you keep track of the intensity of the contractions, noting whether they last 30 seconds or more and if the intervals between them become shorter.

Although the uterine muscle is an involuntary muscle—like your heart or stomach—it is affected by your emotions. Just as you feel your heart beating violently if you are frightened or upset, or your stomach "turning over" if you are very nervous, so your uterus also reacts to anxieties. If you become very excited and tense, it may contract repeatedly—but, unfortunately, with no results. Therefore, your understanding of the process of labor will help you immensely in approaching your delivery. You can avoid unnecessary tension and allow your body to work smoothly during your labor. This understanding and knowledge will also help you give the doctor an accurate description of what's happening when you contact him at the onset of labor. (Your physician will always give you exact instructions as to when he wants to be called and when he wants you to leave for the hospital.)

BREAKING OF WATER

Breaking of water, or rupturing the membranes that contain the amniotic fluid in which the baby lives during your pregnancy, may occur at any time during your labor. You may become aware of a slow leaking or feel a sudden gush of fluid. This amniotic fluid is transparent and is therefore easily distinguishable from urine. You may have noticed, toward the end of your pregnancy, that you occasionally have difficulty in controlling your urine. A sudden sneeze, a laugh or cough can make it difficult for you to hold back the urine. But you *can* control it, whereas if your membranes leak, you cannot stop the escaping fluid by contracting your muscles. This will be a positive indication that the fluid you are losing is amniotic fluid and not urine. (Since your membranes may break while you are in bed, it's a good idea to put a rubber or plastic sheet on your mattress about a week before your due date.)

I'm sure your doctor will have given you instructions to call him as soon as your membranes break. He'll probably ask you to go to the hospital immediately, even if you have not yet felt any contractions. He wants you under hospital care so that no infection can occur once the membranes are ruptured.

Let me assure you that breaking of the membranes is entirely painless and that there is no definite time when you will lose this amniotic fluid. It's even possible that your physician will have to break the bag of waters artificially during your labor.

If your membranes break early in labor, it does not mean that you will have a "dry labor." Actually the fluid that you lose at the beginning of labor is only the tiny amount between the widest diameter of the baby's head and the cervix. Most of the fluid will be plugged off by the baby's head and shoulders. Don't worry if additional water escapes from time to time, especially during a contraction. The uterus keeps making more water, so there will be plenty left for the baby to remain cushioned and to help it finally emerge.

WHAT TO DO WHEN
CONTRACTIONS BEGIN

If contractions start at night and are mild and far apart, try to rest as much as possible. Sleep between contractions as much as you can, so that you are well rested when your labor becomes more active and demands undivided attention. You can be sure that strong, advanced contractions will keep you awake, so make the most of your rest and ignore the beginning of labor as long as you can.

It may be impossible to sleep, however. That's very understandable, too. After all, you have been waiting anxiously for this moment for a long time. But I suggest that you do not lie awake in the dark. Get out of bed and take a comfortable bath in relaxing warm water. If the bath has been banned, take a shower. Then go to the kitchen and make yourself some tea and drink it with lots of sugar or honey. The tea is a stimulant and the sugar is energy-giving. If, after all this activity, you find that labor is progressing—the contractions are increasing in frequency and intensity—you will have to be up anyhow. If, on the other hand, your contractions have slowed down again and there seems to be little change in their character, go back to bed and sleep. You'll probably be very tired in the middle of the night, and sleep may come fairly easily once you have reassured yourself that you can be in control of the situation. Don't wake your husband until you need his help and support. He will better be able to do his part if he is well rested, too.

If labor starts during the day, cut down your intake of food and fluids.

May I suggest that you prepare some Jello a few days before your due date and keep it in the refrigerator. Jello is an ideal snack early in labor. Should you become hungry, broth and light food such as fruit or crackers will also help you if the beginning of labor is long. Do not drink any more milk. Remember that milk is a whole food and that it is hard to digest once labor has started.

Once labor has started in earnest your digestive system automatically stops working. Anything you eat remains undigested in the stomach. I am sure you have noticed even now, during your pregnancy, how distressed you can feel after a meal. There simply is not enough space any more. You can imagine how much more uncomfortable it will be if your stomach stops working. A full stomach may cause vomiting during labor. And should you for any reason require an inhalation anesthetic, it will be infinitely easier to have it on an empty stomach.

I'd like to suggest here that for about one to two weeks before your due date, you have your last meal of the day no later than 7:30 or 8:00 P.M.—and avoid midnight snacks.

Do not immediately lie down when labor begins. If you had a good night's rest go on with your regular activities without tiring yourself. Call your husband home, if he has already left for work. It will be much nicer for you to have him there than to wonder whether he can make it back in time to take you to the hospital.

Do not start any deliberate breathing during contractions until you absolutely feel the need for it. As long as you can walk or talk through a contraction, there is no need to use any specific breathing technique. You'll probably feel a strong temptation to start the deliberate breathing too early, out of pure enthusiasm and excitement that you are at long last in labor. But labor will seem endless if you start controlling it before there is any actual need. You'll tire yourself needlessly, wasting valuable energy that you'll need once labor progresses and the contractions demand concentrated control. Always remember that you must channel your energies, and that from the beginning to the end of your labor you will use the techniques that you have learned, deliberately and with considerable self-discipline.

WHAT TO TAKE
TO THE HOSPITAL

Pack your suitcase at least two weeks before due date. If you're going to nurse the baby, pack two nursing bras. Be sure that you do not buy nursing bras that come with a protective pad. These pads are usually made of some kind of plastic and do not allow for ventilation. The hospital will provide you with gauze pads for protection. (You can buy boxes of these pads at any drugstore, but you might find it cheaper to use old handkerchiefs or cut up an old sheet once you're home again.) Put two or three shorty nightgowns into your suitcase and, if you plan to nurse, be sure that the nightgowns open in front. This will enable you to nurse your baby without having to slip out of your nightgown at each feeding. Pack two belts for your sanitary napkins (the napkins themselves will be provided by the hospital) and a robe and slippers. Do not use tampons until you've had your post-partum examination and your doctor has given you permission. Have a separate bag ready for clothes and diapers for the baby. Put out the clothes you want to wear going home, so your husband won't have a last-minute search through closets and drawers. And don't expect to fit into your tightest skirts or dresses right away.

CONTENTS OF
THE LAMAZE BAG

Do you remember the Lamaze bag I told you to take to the hospital? Here is the list of things to put into your Lamaze bag:

1. A bottle of champagne or wine to celebrate with doctors and nurses after you've given birth. Also bring some plastic glasses, for there are never enough in the hospital. Ask the nurse to put the champagne on ice when you arrive at the hospital, so it will be nice and cool when you need it.

2. Some food for your partner or coach. This is especially useful if you happen to labor at night. Few hospitals have food at nightime, and your partner will get ravenously hungry, because he is working every moment of your labor with you. Luckily, you yourself will not be hungry during labor; also, you won't be allowed to eat. But once you've given birth, you will probably be very hungry. So tell your partner to save a sandwich for you.

3. Some lollipops or peppermint sticks to suck on between contractions if you find that your mouth has become dry from the rapid superficial breathing. Generally you will not be allowed to drink water during labor, though you might be given a little crushed ice or be allowed to rinse your mouth. A lollipop or peppermint stick will feel good and even give you a little sugar.

4. A washcloth or a small sponge. Your husband can wet the washcloth or sponge and refresh your face. He can even let you suck on the wet sponge a little when your mouth gets dry.

5. A chapstick. Your lips may become very dry in labor, and your lipstick is usually not greasy enough to

keep them well lubricated. A chapstick will feel good and also stay on longer than lipstick.

6. A small paper bag to breathe in in case you hyperventilate.

7. A small can of talcum powder to smooth the skin when you or your partner massages your abdomen or any other part of your body.

8. Tennis balls or a can of tennis balls for counter pressure, should you have back labor.

9. Cool pack or Scotch ice to freeze the lower back, also in case you have back labor.

10. Mouth spray to freshen the breath.

11. Anything else you feel like putting in for practical reasons, for fun, or as a "security blanket."

Do not put this Lamaze bag into your suitcase. Your suitcase will probably be taken immediately to the room that you will occupy once you have given birth. Carry it separately or let your husband bring it to you once he comes to the labor room.

ARRIVING AT THE HOSPITAL

When you arrive at the hospital, you will usually have to go first to the admitting office. In some hospitals your partner can attend to the registration or you can even register weeks before you actually enter the hospital. Be sure to bring any necessary insurance cards along and perhaps your checkbook. Some hospitals ask for a deposit when you arrive if you haven't given them one at early registration. Of course they will always admit you, even if you've forgotten to bring a check, but it will cause less trouble at the time if you have it along.

Should you have a contraction while signing forms, don't hesitate to let the clerk wait until you have been able to control it with the appropriate breathing techniques and it has ended. Don't feel embarrassed when stopping in the middle of signing your name. After all, you are the one who is in labor at the moment, not the young woman who sits behind the desk!

You'll then be taken to the labor room, while your husband is asked to remain temporarily in the waiting room. In many hospitals your partner can stay with you when you first arrive at the hospital. It used to be that you were more or less immediately separated, once you entered the hospital, and reunited only after all examinations and "prepping" had been done. I think hospital authorities these days have come to realize that entering a hospital in labor is the first real crisis you have had to cope with. Any hospital stay is anxiety producing. But if your partner can stay with you, you will feel comforted and happy, not only to have him with you later in labor, but also at the beginning when you are being checked, examined and settled into the labor room.

You will undress completely and put on a hospital gown, a shorty which fastens in the back. This is not attractive but is quite practical. The nurse will ask you to give her a urine specimen, and she will take your temperature and your blood pressure. Then either your own doctor or a resident doctor will come and examine you. He will listen to the fetal heart, and check your heart and lungs. He will also ask you when your labor started, whether your membranes have broken, when you ate last, what you ate, etc. In many hospitals a nurse will take a blood sample to re-check your blood type, even though your doctor has done this previously at one of your prenatal visits. The doctor will then examine you internally, either rectally or vaginally. During this examination you should lie flat on your back, breathing deeply with your mouth open. This first internal examination is really most important for you. It will be the first signpost on your journey to the baby's birth. You will probably have been in labor at home for some hours, and no doubt will be eager to find out how much progress you've made so far. Your doctor may examine you during or between contractions. Be sure to ask the doctor how far you have effaced and dilated. Your own doctor will always communicate your progress to you, but don't be surprised if a resident physician seems reluctant to tell you this information. He doesn't know you personally and may not be aware that you are so well prepared for labor and delivery.

After this examination, a nurse will come and "prep" you. Recently a number of hospitals have started to change this procedure a little. They only clip the pubic hair and shave the anal hair. In some hospitals, neither "prep" nor enema are given anymore. You should tell your doctor beforehand that you prefer this kind of partial prepping, or no prepping at all.

It's a good idea to tell the nurse, before she starts to look after you, that you are going to use the Lamaze method. Be sure to ask her not to interrupt while you are using the breathing techniques, but explain that you will be glad to answer any questions as soon as the contraction is over. You will find the nurses most co-operative and helpful. They are usually fascinated at your being able to stay in control so efficiently.

The nurse will also give you an enema if the doctor has ordered one. During the enema breathe deeply, again through your mouth. In many hospitals you will be allowed to expel the enema on a toilet. In others you will be given a bedpan. Should you have to expel the enema on a bedpan, ask the nurse to place it on the edge of the bed and put a chair under the bed so that you can rest your feet and sit upright. Hospital beds are high and it is easy to place a chair under the bed. It is far more comfortable to expel in this way rather than having the pan placed in the middle of your bed. Stay on the toilet or bedpan for at least 20 minutes. If you don't give yourself enough time, you may find that with any subsequent contraction you will lose more stool and have to ask for another bedpan. Do not let anybody hurry you and continue with your breathing techniques whenever you have a contraction.

Now you are ready to ask the nurse to call your partner. (If you know beforehand that your partner cannot stay with you during this preliminary period, tell him ahead of time that the waiting period while you are being examined and "prepped" may be from 45 minutes to one hour. This is important for him to know, since an hour may seem a very long time to him. He may worry unduly or be afraid that he has been forgotten.)

Again, remind your partner to bring a sandwich or some cookies to eat in the hospital. He may get very hungry during your labor and it may be at night when all the coffee shops are closed. Or he may feel that he does not want to leave you alone to get a snack, even for half an hour. Alas, no matter how hungry you may feel, no eating is permitted during labor!

Ask the nurse to roll your bed up to any angle that suits you. You will have to experiment a little. Don't hesitate to ask for another pillow should you need it. If there is no second pillow available, ask the nurse for a blanket which she can roll up or fold to put wherever you need support. Most women feel far more comfortable in an upright position. The breathing is easier this way, and psychologically you will feel far more in control of the situation. The only time you'll have to lie down is when the doctor examines you, or if he feels that a certain position will be better for your labor.

BREATHING
WITH YOUR LABOR

Remember that no labor will follow an exact textbook pattern. There is simply no way to plan in advance what breathing you will use at any given time. The great advantage of the Lamaze method is that you have acquired techniques to use as your labor demands from moment to moment. Do not anticipate a strict pattern, but react to the sensations that you feel at the time. Every labor is different from all others; it is up to you to adjust to your labor as it occurs. However, here are some fundamental rules to keep in mind:

1. Do not start any controlled breathing until you feel the absolute need for it.
2. Stay with the slow chest breathing as long as you can. It's much less fatiguing than the shallow, rapid breathing.
3. If you feel contractions in your back, ask your partner or the nurse to put pressure on your lower spine. You can massage or put pressure on yourself if necessary. Change positions to alleviate the discomfort of back labor by:

a. Sitting upright, leaning slightly forward so that the weight of the baby falls forward.

b. Lying on your side, placing the upper knee in front of the lower one. Place a pillow under the upper knee so that there is no strain on your thigh muscles.

c. Using the knee-chest position to take the pressure off your back.

d. Kneeling and leaning against the raised head of the bed.

4. Ask your partner to help you stay well relaxed. He must remind you to release your arms, legs, or shoulders or face whenever they get tense. You'll find that your homework pays off well here and that you will obey his commands automatically. This will give you both a feeling of doing a difficult job together.

5. Ask your partner to time the contractions and call out the intervals, 15 . . . 30 . . . 45 seconds. This will define and circumscribe the contractions. Once he calls out 45 seconds, you will know that the contraction will not go on much longer. Your beginning cleansing breath will be your husband's cue that the contraction has started. Occasionally it will be difficult for you to know exactly when the contraction has started. Your partner can help you in this case by putting his hand on the fundus, at the top of your uterus. He will usually be able to feel the tightening of the uterus with his fingers before you feel the actual sensation. He can then call out "Now!" and you can follow this command with your cleansing breath and breathing technique. Your partner should encourage and praise you, watching to see that you perform well. We all need encouragement, love and support during labor, especially when we are awake and actively participating in childbirth.

Frequently a fetal monitor is used either externally or internally on you almost as soon as you enter the hospital. This valuable machine monitors the fetal heartbeat, even during contractions, and at the same time shows the intensity of the uterine contractions on a paper on which a pen shows the curve pattern of the contraction. The external monitor is attached to your abdomen by two wide, elastic stockinette belts. This may make effleurage difficult, though you could confine the massage to the lower abdomen, where it is probably most beneficial anyway. The internal monitor will be attached by means of a small electrode to the presenting part of the baby, once the membranes have ruptured.

I would like to include a few words about the fetal monitor here. It is an electronic machine which assures a great safety factor for the baby during labor, as it points into the directions the staff should look if fetal heart irregularities occur.

THE FETAL MONITOR

The machine is invaluable for high-risk mothers or babies. If it is used, even though you may not be a high-risk mother, use it as an added indicator—almost like using biofeedback—to recognize the beginning, strength and end of a contraction. This makes it possible to stay with contractions, catch them on time with breathing techniques, in short, ride the waves. You will be able to watch a paper emerge from the monitor and follow the pen that is drawing the exact curve of your uterine contraction. In fact, you will find that the machine registers your contractions before you are actually aware of them.

It's important that you urinate whenever necessary during the first stage of labor. A large accumulation of urine may become quite uncomfortable and a full bladder takes up precious space in the abdominal cavity. You may find it a little difficult to urinate if the bladder is too full or if the uterus presses on it more and more as the baby descends. If you've had no medication, your husband can help you to the bathroom. If, however, you have had some sedation, ask the nurse for a bedpan.

Your doctor will examine you periodically during labor to determine what progress has been made. Always remember to ask your doctor about your progress after each examination. If he tells you how many centimeters you have dilated, it will give you a rough idea of how far along you've come. From time to time a nurse will listen to the fetal heart or watch the fetal monitor and take your blood pressure. This listening is important, as it is the only way the doctor and nurse can keep in touch with your baby during labor, and be sure that all is well.

THE USE OF MEDICATION

If at any time you should feel the need for medication or sedation, don't hesitate to ask for it. Your doctor will be happy to give you as much relief as he considers medically safe. If he himself suggests medication, he undoubtedly has good reasons for his decision, and I am sure he will explain and discuss them with you.

You've had many months during your prenatal visits to the doctor to discuss your and your partner's active participation in the birth of your child. Any medication he may give you will be necessary to insure both the health of your baby and your own safety. Even if you cannot be awake for the birth of your baby, your control and cooperation will help you cope with labor with less analgesia or anesthesia than you would ordinarily need.

BEGINNING TO PUSH

If you are expecting your first baby, you will probably begin the second stage of labor, or expulsion of the baby, in the labor room. As I have emphasized before, *you must not push* until the doctor has given you permission to push. If you have forgotten how to push, let your husband supervise you. You will probably find that after one or two pushing contractions you will be able to follow the instructions that you have been given. Do not forget to take your pillows to the delivery room so that your head and back can be raised on the delivery table.

It is generally assumed that every woman will have an overwhelming urge to push once she is fully dilated. This is not always so. The majority of women do feel the strong expulsive urge; I have found that the urge to push varies in intensity from woman to woman. There are also some women who never feel any urge whatsoever. The latter may be due to the position or the rotation of the baby. Should you be one of those who does not feel the urge to push and your doctor tells you to push with the next contraction, don't argue, "But I don't feel like it yet." Accept your physician's orders at the time without questioning, and use the pushing technique with the next contraction regardless of whether you feel like it or not.

In the delivery room, your partner will have to wear a cap, gown and mask. He will be told to stand next to your head and not to move from there unless he is asked to do so by your physician. You will be draped, and must remember to keep your hands firmly on the handles or stirrups. Remember, do not touch any of the sterile sheets. Before you start to push on the delivery table, the nurse will pour some disinfectant over your pubic area. This will feel icy cold, but it is actually quite a refreshing surprise!

YOUR BABY ARRIVES!

Your doctor will give you the command to push, once you are on the table. Be sure to pant or blow out whenever he asks you to stop pushing. This allows the doctor time to ease the baby along; he helps deliver the head and shoulders, receiving the rest of the baby's body, which then slips out easily into his hands.

And so you have given birth to your baby! Your doctor will hold the baby up by its feet in order to drain the mucus from its mouth and nose. At this point your baby will cry heartily.

Babies do not come out looking washed and immaculate. Your baby will be wet and wrinkled. It will have patches of a whitish cream all over its body, which is the protective coating, or "vernix," which the baby had while growing in your uterus, and it will look bluish gray for a few seconds before it starts to cry and the color of its skin changes to pink. Black babies will look very light when born. This pigmentation occurs gradually.

Your doctor will then put the baby on your abdomen. Remember, this is the sterile area, therefore an excellent place to put the baby while the umbilical cord is clamped and cut. But keep your hands under the drapes. You will have to wait just a little longer before you are allowed to hold your child.

Once the cord has been cut—which does not hurt either you or the baby—the nurse will wrap it in a warm blanket and put it into a bassinette, which is slightly tilted to help the baby expel more mucus and make breathing easier. The nurse will put a plastic identification band on the baby and on you. Your fingerprints may be taken and possibly the baby's footprints. A few drops of silver nitrate may be put into the baby's eyes, or the baby may be given a penicillin shot instead.

A number of physicians and midwives adopt some of Dr. Leboyer's ideas these days. Also, many couples are asking that Leboyer's approach, i.e., "the baby is a person," be used. Lights are dimmed in the delivery room, except for a spotlight on the mother's pelvic floor. The baby stays for a longer period on the mother's abdomen so that she can touch it gently, rub its back and establish eye contact with her child.

At this point you will be given an injection of a hormone which helps expel the placenta, contract the uterus and prevent excessive bleeding. In the meantime, you may have another contraction. The doctor will feel your uterus and decide that it is time for you to "express" the placenta (our third stage of labor). Be sure to help the doctor with another good push to expel the placenta. The doctor will assist you by putting gentle pressure on your abdomen. It will take no more than two to three minutes to expel the placenta. Now your hard work is over.

If he has performed an episiotomy, your doctor will clean you up and perform "the repair" or stitching. While he is doing this ask to hold your baby. Frequently you'll get to hold and talk to it while your doctor does the repair. Your husband will also hold and touch the baby and help you put the baby to your breast should you desire to nurse it right there and then.

Your partner's place is always next to you, so that he can talk to you, helping to raise your head and shoulders when you push. Under no circumstances should he look over the doctor's shoulder unless he is actually asked to come to the doctor's side.

AFTER YOU'VE GIVEN BIRTH

For about two hours after you have given birth, a nurse will watch you closely. She will massage your abdomen from time to time to make sure that your uterus remains firm. Occasionally the nurse will show you how to massage your abdomen yourself.

Now you will be taken back to your own bed in your own room. You will probably feel fantastically elated! You may not be able to sleep much the first night after you've given birth. You'll be proud of your baby and of yourself, of your husband and of your ability to have functioned so well.

However, there is still some immediate work ahead of you. Do not forget to do your pelvic floor contractions; they will speed your recovery. Also you *will* experience some slight continued contractions, which are a good sign that your uterus is healing and contracting again to its original size. These contractions after childbirth will be more pronounced if this was your second, third or fourth delivery, since it becomes more difficult for the muscles to regain their original tone. You are also likely to feel them when you nurse your baby.

Please remember that these contractions occur for a very good reason: to get your uterus back to its usual size. They are a sign of a speedy recovery.

And so you have given birth to your baby. You have joined all the thousands of mothers and fathers who have trained themselves to give birth actively instead of passively, and you have prepared yourself diligently for the first step on the road to successful parenthood.

A
MOTHER'S
REPORT

BY PHYLIS FEINSTEIN

*A personal, moment-by-moment account
by a young woman, prepared with the
Lamaze method, of her first childbirth*

The beginning of my labor was less than auspicious. My first indication that the baby would be born this year yet occurred Tuesday around 1:30 P.M. when my mucous plug came out. No contractions, no showing . . . nothing.

All afternoon I waited. About once every half hour I'd get a tiny tweak in my pelvic area, but it was so short and inconsequential that I'm still not sure I didn't wish it into existence. I called Richard, my husband, a dozen times during the course of the day to tell him not to come home yet. However, I also informed him it could happen any minute.

For some reason every appliance in our house got serviced that Tuesday. And so the washing machine got its new grounding wire, the dryer a new catch, etc. I was busy answering the door all afternoon, feeling fine—if a little apprehensive. Checking my preparation for when labor would begin, I found a half bowl of Jello in the refrigerator (if I should get hungry during the earliest stages), a container of stew in the freezer (for Richard to take to the hospital in a wide-mouthed thermos in case *he* got hungry), my luggage packed and my Lamaze goodie bag complete.

About the goodie bag: I had decided to make it particularly nice, figuring that at the time I would need it, any pleasantry would help. And so the bag itself was not an ordinary brown, dull grocery model. This was a slick-papered pink (prophetic) bag, the kind lazy gift-givers use instead of fancy wrapping paper on the outside of presents. Inside was a brand-new flowered washcloth—blue (unprophetic)—my favorite talc (we used practically the entire can), chap-stick, some fancy lollipops, and the three-dollar-wonder of a clock I used to time my breathing exercises. The clock has a cracked face, no minute hand, but the niftiest second hand. I was confidently prepared . . . until 3:00 A.M. Wednesday morning, when the first real contraction lifted me out of a deep sleep. I bolted from my warm bed groaning, "My God, I've got back labor." Naturally this woke Richard, and for the next half hour all the careful planning, the long, intellectual discussions about not panicking were forgotten.

We were both in a maddening state of hysteria. I couldn't face having back labor.

Richard couldn't face that I was in labor and, after assuring me labor doesn't start this way, he said in his most condescending tone, "Obviously, you're constipated." Then he added, "Gee, I'm starving," and dove into the refrigerator.

Meanwhile I sat on a kitchen stool, effleuraging like mad, breathing properly and quietly swearing alternately at back labor and at my husband. I soon checked my contractions at five-minute intervals, when I mustered, "Richard, you'd better call the doctor."

Richard acquiesced. In his Cary Grant manner he began the conversation suavely, "Hello, Doctor. How are you?" (At 3:00 in the morning!) "Yes, this is Richard Feinstein. Phylis thinks she's in labor. Every five minutes. Clock them for another half hour and if they are steady call back? Call back anyway? O.K."

By fifteen minutes later the contractions were coming every four minutes. We called our doctor again and were told to come nearer the hospital (we live half an hour away) and wait a bit at my cousin's, who lives only a block from the hospital. We forgot Richard's stew. But before we left he ate my Jello. And while I dressed he managed to brew some tea and pack some fruit for the trip. By this time I had hold of myself, and found the ride on the parkway uneventful. Richard concentrated on the road and I on my contractions. I cracked open the package of lollipops and lapped away when my mouth became dry. (First mistake: Don't buy sweet pops. The smaller, sourer ones are much better.)

I had beside me two pillows I'd grabbed just in case the hospital was short-stocked. It proved to be good thinking!

We arrived at my cousin's at 4:00 A.M. The door was opened by two sleepy and excited relatives. Now my contractions were two minutes apart. Another call to the doctor and we were off to the hospital at last. We entered, Richard carrying my goodie bag and his box lunch and I clutching my pillows and sucking my too-sweet lollipop. We were quite a pair.

An o.b. nurse was sent down to accompany me to the maternity floor. In the elevator she looked me up and down, taking in my pillows and lollipop.

"Why those?" She pointed.

I said, "Pillows for back support. Pops for dry mouth."

Off the elevator she headed me toward a room I shared with three other ladies. I readied for bed and, in between shallow breathing techniques, I asked a nurse to roll up my bed.

She did, muttering, "Everyone lies down for labor, you sit like a tailor sewing."

She left as Richard returned from signing me in. He dismantled the bag, placing the talc, washcloth, chapstick and lollies close by. The doctor arrived, followed by a blonde bulldozer of a nurse. She looked at Richard and said, "Better you wait in the solarium. Better still wait downstairs till it's over." In unison Richard and I said, "No, he's going to stay." The nurse aimed her attack at the doctor. "You know the rules—husbands stay only by special permission of the hospital president."

"Fine," said Dr. H. "Call Harvey."

She: "Harvey" (the name stuck in her throat) "doesn't like being called at 4:30 A.M."

Dr. H.: "He's been called before. Let's talk about this."

And they stepped around my tent and left the room. Richard timed my contractions; I rubbed my belly.

Ten minutes later, Dr. H. came back and broke my water. I was put on a movable table and taken to a private room, where Richard and I spent the entire labor.

We were finally settled and ready for action. For the first time I had a chance to evaluate what was happening inside me. I wasn't having true back labor because, Dr. H. assured me, the baby was not in a posterior position. The contractions began at the back, reached their peak about three inches below my navel and then spread in both directions toward my hips as they subsided. I was breathing as directed in the second stage of the first part of labor (dilation)—cleansing breath, slow breath, acceleration as the contraction built and then regaining a slow pace as it lessened. The doctor examined me at 5:30 and told us the good news. I was 5½ centimeters dilated. Richard was busy indeed sprinkling on talc, pouring water on my tongue and lips, applying chapstick. I would point and he would do. In between such activities he sat on the chair near the bed and drew me (perhaps the first portrait of a pregnant Lamaze in labor) or surreptitiously snitched a grape from his lunch pail. The doctor left the room, promising to return in an hour. Everything was concentrated on my work. And it *was* work.

The analogy comparing the contraction control of riding a wave is excellent. And once I caught the "wave" and rode it until it broke quietly on the shores of my conscious being, I smiled. *Smiled* during labor. When I think of pain I think of something sharper, something stabbing. Nothing like that kind of pain happened. I could feel what seemed to be a regular agonizing stretching, very uncomfortable, but with all my breathing and concentration, it was easily bearable! Dr. H. came back at 6:30 and said I was doing fine.

At 7:00 he examined me. The news—8 to 8½ centimeters. I was in transition and I didn't even know it! Contractions were coming at exactly one minute, forty-five seconds. "How much longer?" I hoarsely whispered.

"About two and a half hours." Dr. H. replied. He was off by fourteen minutes!

The new shift of nurses arrived at 7:00. As fate would have it they were the same wonderful group that showed me around the maternity floor a month earlier. What a cheering section they turned out to be! They breathed with me, came in between their duties to encourage me, were in the delivery room when Amanda was born. Dr. H. never left the room from 7:00 on. Just letting us know that he was very much a part of what was going on by being there. The only time he asked me if I wanted any medication was about 4:30 A.M. He said it to reassure me, I guess. But he never offered it again. Even when the going got tough during the last stage of transition. After the birth, I asked why he never again mentioned it. His answer: "Who needed it?"

By 8:00 I was 9½ centimeters and fagged out. I wanted to push, but Dr. H. said not yet. I wanted to push very badly. I lost my breathing, grabbed for Richard's and Dr. H's hands, blew out all my good oxygen and squeezed their hands. "It's time," I moaned. Dr. H's examination showed I was wrong. The cervix had just a little left to dilate, enough to make a difference between pushing uselessly and productive expulsion. Meanwhile Richard got me on the road to breathing properly by forcing me to listen to him do it. Thirty minutes later came the word—*push!* They rolled down the bed. I got into position (after Richard reminded me to get into position) and I pushed. Erroneously I thought three good pushes and out would come baby. Ha!

The hardest part, for me, was the expulsion. It hurt and I was tired. "No more pushing," I groaned, just as the doctor said, "Come here, Richard—here comes your baby's head and the hair's black." Rich rushed around the bed. Then I grinned and said, "Who's tired?" I wanted to push more than anything else in the world.

They took us to the delivery room. Dr. H. administered a local for the episiotomy. What seemed like five pushes—good ones—and then minutes later the doctor lifted up the biggest, most beautiful girl baby I've ever seen: 8 pounds, 2 ounces, 21 inches of Lamaze testimonial.

I don't know words to describe it.

A
FATHER'S
REPORT

BY PATRICK CASEY

*The role of the husband is crucial
throughout labor and delivery; here
is one man's report of his experience*

The birth of our first child had been an unpleasant experience. My wife had no real idea of what to expect when those first contractions came four years ago. She was surprised, frightened and extremely uncomfortable. Neither of us had any notion that childbirth could be such a harrowing ordeal. After a few moments of desperate handholding I was asked to leave the hospital room; she was heavily medicated and, at the end of several hours of anxiety and confusion, I was informed that our first son had arrived. Happily, he was a fine, healthy baby, but the experience was so distressing that for a long time Marilyn would not consider going through the whole thing again.

Eventually we did decide to have another child. About the same time Marilyn become pregnant again a friend told us about a marvelous new technique of childbirth called the Lamaze Method. A clear idea of what happens physically during labor and delivery, a few exercises to prepare the body, a system of breathing to alleviate discomfort during contractions and a supporting role for the husband—it sounded practical, worth investigating. Certainly we wanted to do something to avoid another traumatic experience, so we went to an obstetrician who encouraged the Lamaze Method and enrolled in the six-lesson course.

Those weekly sessions were really quite marvelous. Not only did they lift the traditional veil of mystery about childbirth by simply explaining what was going to happen and how to prepare for it, but they helped eliminate any nervous apprehension about the whole event. By creating a warm atmosphere of rational discussion, and by giving us specific exercises and techniques to practice together, the classes gradually dispelled our anxieties. We aired our questions with the other four couples in the class; we worked together at home; we arranged with the doctor and hospital that I be allowed to be with Marilyn in the labor and delivery room. The whole thing became a happy collaboration, something we were preparing for as husband and wife.

The first contractions came at about 3:00 A.M. a few days after the anticipated date of delivery. Marilyn woke me at 3:30, announcing that she had been having what "could be real contractions" for half an hour. By 4 A.M. I was calling Dr. A. to report regular mild contractions about five minutes apart. We knew that a second baby usually comes faster than the first, but we were surprised to hear him tell us to get down to the hospital as quickly as we could. Marilyn's suitcase and the little Lamaze bag had both been carefully packed weeks before. Without further delay we hopped in a cab.

Marilyn's water hadn't broken yet—the first thing that happened when Jonathan was born—but as we sped toward the hospital her contractions continued to be definite and regular. I suggested that she begin the first breathing technique, but she refused, reminding me that we had been taught to wait until it was absolutely necessary. At 4:30 we pulled up to the night entrance of the hospital.

We had registered and left a deposit with the hospital a month before, so we went straight up to the fourth-floor delivery area where Dr. A. was already waiting. In a wonderfully paternal manner he took Marilyn into the labor room to be dressed and examined while I changed into regulation sterile-white shirt and pants next door. About ten minutes later I joined Marilyn in the labor room, where one pillow was under her head and another under her knees. She told me that she was already 5 centimeters dilated and would allegedly have the baby within the hour. It was now 4:45 A.M. We were both terribly excited as she began doing the accelerated breathing. I made myself useful by powdering her abdomen and giving her a lollipop to suck on between contractions. Marilyn laughed at my hospital get-up. She thought it would be a girl. I was noncommittal.

A friendly nurse bustled in and out, while a resident technician took a sample of blood. The contractions had been mild and relatively close together, but now were getting slightly stronger and more difficult to control. It was exactly like our practice at home: Marilyn breathed and concentrated on a spot across the little room, while I called off fifteen-second intervals of the contraction.

At 5:10 things quickened; Marilyn began having really strong contractions. Immediately we shifted into the rapid breathing and blowing method of breathing. The doctor came in, made a quick examination and called for the nurse; we were going into the delivery room! I grabbed two pillows and tried to keep up with the rolling table, while fitting on my cap and face mask. The nurse laughed at me as I trotted along, dropping a pillow every three feet, but dauntlessly following everyone into the delivery room where Marilyn was already being transferred to the table. Now the contractions were quite intense and she really had to hold back the urge to push and force herself to concentrate on breathing.

The atmosphere in the delivery room was something like a congenial clubhouse. I was introduced to the anesthesiologist ("He's here just in case we need any medication.") and to the two nurses who were performing little chores about the room with towels and instruments. The baby's head was about to show, the doctor told us, and with the next contraction he would break the membranes and Marilyn could at last begin to push. I mopped her brow, which really wasn't at all necessary, and tried to keep busy arranging the pillows beneath her head.

"Ready," Dr. A. said quietly, as Marilyn took her two deep breaths, held the third and pushed. A fierce growl-like noise filled the room as she bared her teeth, straining down and out, gripping the metal bars of the table. I think she must have been oblivious to everything else in the room, so powerful was her concentration and determination. A gush of water shot across the room.

"Good!" the doctor said, ". . . and again . . ."

The incredible noise she made! And the strength of her face. It was like watching some legendary hero perform a Herculean triumph, toppling a temple, overthrowing a false god, defeating an enemy.

"Very good! Come and look—you can see the baby's hair."

I rushed to peer over the doctor's shoulder. There was the top of the baby's head, plastered with what looked then like dark hair.

Marilyn gave a faint smile and prepared to push again. At this point the doctor gave Marilyn an injection of local anesthetic and made an incision, painlessly, to enlarge the opening. One last push and I saw the head come completely out. Dr. A. worked his hand under the shoulder and in a second the whole child slid easily into the world.

"It's a boy!" the anesthesiologist said, first to notice from his vantage point at Marilyn's head. "The time is 5:37."

It was indeed a boy, looking quite wrinkled and angry. Being a naturally anxious sort, I was relieved to note that he had only one head, two arms, two legs, etc. His skin had a bluish tinge, as he hung from the doctor's grip, and his little body was tense. The umbilical cord ran from his navel to the placenta, which had not yet been expelled. The cord was clamped and cut, while I fretted about his lifeless appearance. The doctor then gave him a slap on the soles of his feet. (Apparently, spanking the bottom is only for the movies.) There was a gurgle deep in the baby's throat, in another second a faint cry, and then a series of lusty yells and wails. He was really alive—very much so!

Dr. A. ordered another short push to expel the placenta, and in no time at all he had stitched up the episiotomy. In the meantime, we could not take our eyes off little Peter Nicholas (for that was to be his name), who was getting pinker and pinker in the glass box he had been placed in next to the delivery table. We could see now that what I had thought was dark hair was really wet red hair, exactly the same shade as his mother's and brother's.

Then we were left quite alone. The anesthesiologist packed up his tanks and left. The nurses were in and out, and the doctor went off to see about another woman who had arrived in labor.

It was the proudest, happiest moment of our lives. Here was our new son, after only two hours of mild labor and absolutely no medication whatsoever, not even an aspirin! The difference between this and our first childbirth was miraculous. Marilyn had used the Lamaze Method to perfection. The method had given us calmness with which we both approached the event, confidence with which we were able to cope with each succeeding stage, joy in doing all this together, and this ultimate, happy reward.

ABOUT THE AUTHOR

ELISABETH BING was born in Berlin, Germany, of a distinguished scientific family. She was trained as a physical therapist in London, England, and came to New York in 1949. She worked under Dr. Alan Guttmacher in the Childbirth Education Program at the Mt. Sinai Hosital from 1952 until 1960. Elisabeth Bing became one of the co-founders of the American Society for Psychoprophylaxis in Obstetrics, Inc. in 1960. Since then she has continued her hospital work at the Flower and Fifth Avenue hospitals as instructor in childbirth education for the department of obstetrics and gynecology of the N.Y. Medical College. While continuing her hospital work, Ms. Bing has trained thousands of expectant parents in her own private classes. She has traveled widely all over the U.S. and Europe, giving workshops, lecturing and holding seminars in many colleges, hospitals and communities.